GOING
BROKE

GOING BROKE

Bankruptcy, Business Ethics, and the Bible

John R. Sutherland

Foreword by Wally Kroeker

HERALD PRESS
Waterloo, Ontario
Scottdale, Pennsylvania

Canadian Cataloguing in Publication Data
Sutherland, John R., 1947-
    Going broke : bankruptcy, business ethics, and the Bible

    Includes bibliographical references and index.
    ISBN 08361-3556-3

    1. Finance, Personal—Religious aspects—Christianity.
    2. Bankruptcy—Moral and ethical aspects. 3. Business ethics.
    4. Bankruptcy—Canada. 5. Bankruptcy—United States. I. Title.

    HF5388.S8 1991   261.8'5   C91-093778-8

The paper used in this publication is recycled and meets the minimum requirements of American National Standard for Information Sciences—
Permanence of Paper for Printed Library Materials, ANSI Z39.48-1984.

GOING BROKE
Copyright © 1991 by Herald Press, Waterloo, Ont. N2L 6H7
    Published simultaneously in the United States by Herald Press,
    Scottdale, Pa. 15683. All rights reserved.
Library of Congress Catalog Number: 91-070935
International Standard Book Number: 0-8361-3556-3
Printed in the United States of America.
Book and cover design by Merrill R. Miller.

1 2 3 4 5 6 7 8 9 10 97 96 95 94 93 92 91

Dedicated to my father
Don Sutherland,
and to the memory of my mother,
Reita,
and to my parents-in-law,
Jake and Marjorie Martin

My son, keep your father's commands
and do not forsake your mother's teaching.
For these commands are a lamp,
this teaching is a light.
Proverbs 6:20, 23

Contents

Foreword

A man in a church I once attended lost his home, vehicle, and savings through forced bankruptcy. When he asked the pastor for support, he was urged to step down from two church boards. It seems his business dilemma made him unfit for leadership.

Another victim told me of being ostracized after he lost his business. One fellow Christian would leave church by a side door to avoid having to talk to him.

Such sad cases are not unusual. The Christian church does not always shine its best on members who suffer this degrading fate. It often offers condemnation rather than compassion. That is because bankruptcy is frequently seen as not only a business failure but also a moral failure. Sometimes, to be sure, bankruptcy includes moral failure. But not always. John Sutherland's timely book will help the church and its business community fashion a more redemptive approach to this thorny issue.

As Sutherland shows so well, the malady of bankruptcy is not going away. We hear the latest "body count" in the daily news or at the lunch counter. Every businessperson knows someone who has suffered business failure, and in these uncertain times the threat of it hangs over many others like a sword of Damocles.

Nor are nonbusiness folks immune in this age of reckless debt. Credit experts say the average North American family is only three weeks away from personal bankruptcy. Sooner or later, it could happen to someone close.

This is not only a book about bankruptcy, however. It is also a book about business morality, ethical theory, and Christian discipleship. Chapter 5, for example, is an excellent introduction to the realm of ethical decision making. Sutherland analyzes various moral grids and shows their weaknesses when applied to everyday business problems. He artfully explores what Scripture has to say about pressing issues of justice, property rights, preservation of the family, and care for society's weaker members.

Anyone who lends or borrows money ought to pay careful attention to chapter 7, "What the Bible Teaches About Debt." Concise but thorough, it is as good a treatment as you'll find.

From here Sutherland goes into what Scripture might teach us on the ethics of bankruptcy. Clearly the biblical writers expect people to pay their debts—but this is balanced by such considerations as the need for compassion and the call to cancel debts at periodic intervals (sabbatical and Jubilee years).

"No noble goal is achieved when scrupulous debtors get off scot-free," Sutherland writes. "But the Old Testament political economy did provide for the cancellation of debts as an act of mercy, with no stigma attached."

Sutherland parts company with those who believe bankruptcy is always wrong. But he does not claim it is always right. Many businesses fail because of mismanagement, lack of integrity, greed, and abuse of credit. Although the forgiveness of debt through bankruptcy is a legitimate option, "Christian businesspeople must still see their business involvements as service in God's name—and act accordingly."

Going Broke deserves serious reading by a wide audience. It belongs on every pastor's desk and in every church library. It's great grist for Sunday school or small group discussion. Seasoned executives, as well as young people entering the business world, will have their ethical edge sharpened by the solid moral insights, abundant practical illustrations, and continual encouragement to lodge their career firmly under the lordship of Christ.

Those on the brink of financial ruin will find illumination in chapter 4, "The Bankruptcy Process and Its Alternatives." And any student of Christian business ethics will find the bibliography alone worth the price of the book.

My hat is off to John Sutherland for tackling this difficult topic. *Going Broke* is an important step toward helping working Christians bridge the Sunday-Monday gap. It will help the church become a more faithful and compassionate agent of Christ in a needy world.

—*Wally Kroeker, editor,* The Marketplace
Mennonite Economic Development Associates
Winnipeg, Manitoba

Introduction

Without God, everything is permitted.
—*The Brothers Karamazov,* Dostoevski

Bankruptcy statistics grabbed the headlines in the early 1980s, then faded from public attention as the economy improved. As of this writing, the economy is again weakening and bankruptcy is again being seen as a major problem.

In the 12 months ended June 30, 1989, bankruptcy filings in the United States rose 12.8% to a new one year high of 725, 484 cases, almost triple the recessionary years of 1981 or 1982. In Canada, the number of business and consumer bankruptcies is approaching record levels. The frightening fact is that only one in five business failures shows up in official bankruptcy statistics.

The ethics of bankruptcy are greatly debated. Its horrible impact is not. Consider the turmoil of a Mennonite businessman who ran a highly successful automobile dealership for 40 years.

That evening the banker phones. He wants to see me in my office at eight in the morning.

I meet him. He is there with his lawyer, the receiver, and the bailiff. The lawyer reads the demand. "Can you pay off your loan in the next hour?" How many people could repay their operating loan in that time? I couldn't. There had been no previous mention of foreclosure. The receiver asks me to call my employees together. He fires everyone. The bailiff changes the lock. They take my car. They accompany me to my house to pick up my wife's car. By 9:30 the same day: 40 years of hard work, all my dreams, my future, and my retirement are gone.

I have no income.
I have no place to work.
I have no status.
No one wants me.
Suddenly I realize I have no money. I have no job. The only vehicle I have is a car I bought for my teenage daughter a few months ago. I will lose our home.
Everything I've worked for is gone.
My employees are paid their salaries and vacation pay. I get nothing.
What will I do?
I am angry and ashamed.
I am a failure.
My pride is hurt.
I am disappointed with people, the church, and friends.
I question God, even blame him.
I wonder about my faith.
How much suffering can I take and survive?[1]

Most people acknowledge that bankruptcy can take its emotional and spiritual toll. Many, however, question its ethics—for a variety of reasons. People who subscribe to the "health and wealth gospel" question a bankrupt person's faith or obedience. They assume that business failure is a sure sign that the businessperson is out of God's favor. Other Christians believe the Bible teaches that all debts must be repaid regardless of financial difficulties.

For many people, bankruptcy is, of course, simply a legitimate part of the world of economic affairs. They think it should be seen as a completely acceptable business tactic—regrettable, perhaps, and embarrassing, but in no way shameful or unethical.

Consider Tom, a consultant who declared bankruptcy after his firm floundered, leaving him with debts of $80,000 in deferred taxes and $25,000 for leased office equipment.

Tom discovered that the "social disgrace" of his bankruptcy wasn't such a disgrace after all. For one thing, he kept his mouth shut.

"Obviously I don't talk about the bankruptcy. Not even your closest associates should know about it. People who were not disadvantaged by your bankruptcy shouldn't know about it. Not even your family should know about it if you can possibly avoid it."

There are a person's inner reproaches, of course. By successfully declaring bankruptcy one is, after all, not paying legitimate debts, a lapse most of us have been taught to consider less than honorable.

Tom puts it all in perspective, however. "If you keep the reasons for declaring bankruptcy in mind, and clearly identify your needs, you're halfway to satisfying your own conscience," he maintains.

The "reasons" are that you simply can't pay your debts—and let's face it, extending credit is a business too, and a very profitable one for institutions that specialize in it. (As for Tom's main creditor, the government, Tom says simply, "I've paid enough taxes.")

Tom didn't declare bankruptcy out of panic, or to cheat somebody deliberately. "If you just want to run away from obligations by declaring bankruptcy, it shows," Tom insists. "But if you're simply trying to provide a bridge from insurmountable obligations to new opportunities, then you have to take it as a practical step that's legally available to you."[2]

Contrast this perspective with that of well-known Christian business writer and speaker Larry Burkett.

Now isn't that amazing to you, that somebody would actually default on a debt that they created legally, morally, ethically, and then they would default on it? See, it ought to never happen with Christianity, or it ought to happen so rarely that we would take that person, and we would admonish them according to Matthew 18, and bring them before the church to restore them back to the faith.[3]

My purpose in writing this book is to sort out the ethics of bankruptcy from a Christian perspective. The issue is complex and controversial. To arrive at what I believe are biblically solid conclusions, I will use the following approach.

Chapter 1 introduces the grim scenario of bankruptcy and

business failure. It notes the seeming explosion of filings in both the United States and Canada. Also included is an exploration of the variety of beliefs concerning bankruptcy ethics.

Chapter 2 discusses the very practical problem of how bankruptcy impacts the unfortunate bankrupt both emotionally and spiritually, and how he or she may be helped.

After we examine the extent and human impact of bankruptcy, we will move on in Chapters 3 and 4 to discuss its mechanics. Chapter 3 explains the major causes of both business and personal bankruptcies.

Chapter 4 overviews the evolution of bankruptcy law. Distinctions between voluntary and involuntary bankruptcies, as well as between business and personal bankruptcies, are explained. Alternatives to the process are explored.

Chapters 5-8 move to the ethical analysis. Before we can come to any conclusions about the ethics of bankruptcy, we must talk in more general terms about ethics and how they apply in business life.

Chapter 5 explores the meaning of ethics and various understandings of how to apply proper moral reasoning to business decisions.

Chapter 6 tries to apply ethical theory to everyday business decision-making. In Chapter 7 we study what the Bible teaches about debt.

Drawing on this material, Chapter 8 puts forward an ethical view of bankruptcy which I feel biblical teaching and ethical theory demand.

This book will interest people involved in, or preparing for, the business world. It may be helpful to anyone with a general interest in applied ethics. But I am also trying to provide an important resource for a group who may not know much about business but probably would like to—pastors and other church leaders.

There is little teaching from our pulpits on the relationship between the Bible and economic life. Many preachers and church leaders feel unqualified to teach or give counsel to business people who turn to them for help. Moreover, "gospel of of prosperity" views have frightened many people who are hurting financially from seeking spiritual support where they should most readily find it—their church. Church leaders need resources to gain a clearer understanding of the bankruptcy process, the causes of bankruptcy, and the emotional and spiritual impact of business failure. Then perhaps they can more effectively preach to and counsel people involved in economic life—especially those encountering severe financial difficulties.

—*John R. Sutherland*
Langley, British Columbia

GOING
BROKE

PART I
Bankruptcy: The Economic and Human Cost

He was only eight years old. For him, buying a whole bag of penny candy at once was high finance. Dad was busy, that he knew. Running a manufacturing business meant lots of late suppers, or no supper at all, while the kids spent the evening with their mother. *Bankruptcy* was not a word in his third-grade speller.

Then came the day his mother gave him money to buy bread and milk at the corner store. As he walked out of the front door of their new home—which they were soon to lose, along with the car and furniture—he almost tripped over a bag of groceries. It had mysteriously appeared on the steps.

He asked his dad that night where it had come from. A tired, discouraged father shouted, "Be quiet!" and refused to discuss the matter further.

All this happened 35 years ago. That father is now in happy and relatively prosperous retirement—but he still won't discuss that bag of groceries.

Chapter 1
Bankruptcy: The Grim Scenario

I guess if you have to choose between bankruptcy and
suicide, bankruptcy is the lesser of two evils. At least it
gets you out of debt alive, which your death might not.
  —Mike Grenby, financial columnist

The headline read, "I Had 228 Creditors." Such headlines
have not been unusual in recent years. The 1980s saw rates
of business failure unknown since the Great Depression.
Many business people and other individuals have faced the
specter of bankruptcy and all that it entails. What is telling
about this headline is that it did not appear in the financial
pages or in a business periodical—but on the front cover of a
Sunday school paper.[1]

A growing number of North Americans, including devout
Christians, are encountering serious debt problems. As part
of the drastic growth in personal and business bankruptcies,
many Christian business people have experienced the devastating effects of credit obligations and insufficient cash.
This phenomenon has invited much discussion of whether a
bankruptcy can be a Christian option.

Some commentators are adamant that bankruptcy is no
alternative for the Christian. American businessman and author Albert J. Johnson suggests that those considering voluntary bankruptcy to resolve debt problems should read
Psalm 37:21, "The wicked borrow and do not repay, but the
righteous give generously." He argues that a person considering bankruptcy is in financial trouble because of past violations of scriptural principles.[2]

On the other hand, an editorial in the *Bookstore Journal*, a publication of the Christian Booksellers Association, states that business failure, while embarrassing, is not a sin.[3]

The bankruptcy picture is a grim one indeed. Business bankruptcies in Canada soared from 2,976 in 1976 to 8,055 in 1981 and 10,765 in 1982.

The following table indicates that the numbers are unacceptably high. And if the recession that seemed imminent as this book was being written did hit North America, current bankruptcy statistics are probably much higher.

Canadian business bankruptcies

1983	10,260
1984	9,578
1985	8,663
1986	8,502
1987	7,659
1988	8,031
1989	8,664

Source: Consumer and Corporate Affairs Canada.

Conditions have been similarly gloomy in the U.S.A. Business bankruptcy petitions filed in 1987 exceeded 88,000, a number almost double that of 1981.[4]

"Shocking" is not too strong a word to describe the growth of personal bankruptcies in Canada. The number rose from 1,549 in 1967 (a rate of 7.6 per 100,000 population) to 12,772 in 1977 (54.8 per 100,000) and 17,892 in 1979 (75.5 per 100,000).

Figures from 1980 onward again indicate that personal bankruptcies peaked during the recession of the early 1980s but remain at a troubling level and were rising during the "prosperity" of the late 1980s.

Canadian consumer bankruptcies

1980	21,025
1981	23,036
1982	30,643
1983	26,822
1984	22,022
1985	19,752
1986	21,765
1987	24,384
1988	25,817
1989	29,202

Source: Consumer and Corporate Affairs Canada.

This unexpected rise is characteristic of the U.S. as well. Non-business bankruptcy petitions have shown startling growth in recent years.

1980	241,431
1981	312,914
1982	311,443
1983	304,916
1984	282,105
1985	297,885
1986	401,575
1987	473,000

Source: Statistical Abstract of the United States, 1989. 109th edition, p. 527.

In 1989, an estimated 820,000 Americans filed for bankruptcy. In addition, the International Credit Association maintains that 24 million consumers are in financial trouble, and 3 million are on the verge of filing for bankruptcy.[5]

The financial losses associated with bankruptcy are enormous. For instance in 1986 when 8,502 Canadian businesses and 21,765 consumers went bankrupt creditors claimed $3.2 billion—but the assets actually realized were only $250 million. Wage earners were owed about $30 million because of bankruptcies and *receiverships* (the term used when property is held in trust and administered by someone appointed by the courts, or in some cases by a secured creditor, until the courts establish who owns what).[6]

Bankruptcy statistics tell only part of the story. While estimates vary, insolvency experts agree that counting bankrupts alone as an indication of how the economy is doing would be like measuring only the tips of icebergs. One senior officer of the Canadian Organization of Small Business noted that only *one in five* business failures show up in official bankruptcy statistics.

Only very rarely are there enough [corporate] assets to make it worthwhile for creditors to go after the company. Instead, small companies voluntarily close their doors, are absorbed by larger and more profitable companies, enter into mergers, or fall prey to bank-triggered receiverships.[7]

Statistics can shield us from the human tragedy which often lies behind them. For instance, *The Mennonite Brethren Herald* reported in early 1986 that about 10% of the farmers in Canada and the United States had been bankrupted in the past seven years. Another 15 to 20% were in dire financial straits, unlikely to survive another year without government assistance. The *Herald* called it the worst farming depression since the 1930s.

Included in the report on farm failure was an article by an

obviously deeply devout Mennonite farmer whose 160-acre farm had been in the family for 120 years. But two years of dry weather and bad crops, coupled with doubling interest rates and a poor livestock market, had doomed this treasured family business. The author honestly recorded the havoc this loss was playing with his faith.

> Last night I was reading in Mark 15 how Jesus suffered on the cross. It hit me in a new way. Jesus cried out with a loud voice—that means he shouted at the top of his lungs, "My God, my God, why hast thou forsaken me?" That says it. That captures exactly how I feel. Why has God allowed this to happen to us? Doesn't he care? Why would he let us feel so alone and forsaken? Sometimes I feel like climbing the Harvestore and hollering from the top those same words of Jesus. Am I crazy?[8]

At one time, bankruptcy carried considerable stigma. Albert Johnson notes that during the crash of 1929 many men chose suicide over facing their creditors and bankruptcy.

Such guilt feelings seem to have lessened, however. Johnson quotes the president of San Francisco's American Bankruptcy Council as saying, "There is a new morality. There's no guilt, no feeling of any loss, any shame, nothing. It's just done, period."[9]

Some may dispute the magnitude of the decline, but economic observers admit that the stigma is reduced. For instance, a commentator on the increasing rate of bankruptcies in British Columbia in 1983 said that bankruptcies are rising because the stigma is falling.[10]

The authors of the *1970 Report of the Study Committee on Bankruptcy and Insolvency Legislation* arrived at a similar conclusion. They stated that the underlying assumption of the Canadian Bankruptcy Act is that there is an economic and social stigma attached to bankruptcy. They said that, just a few years before their report was completed, not paying debts was thought shameful. The report noted a changed attitude.

In the case of those for whom the stigma was real, there was an acceptance of responsibility for one's conduct and the results of it. The disgrace of bankruptcy, more than any legal sanction, effectively removed the bankrupt from business and thereby protected both the business community and the public from the incompetent or dishonest businessman. In our modern society . . . there is a tendency to give more weight to those factors that encourage the diminution of the responsibility of the individual. It is also becoming apparent that there is an increasing number of persons who more readily accept bankruptcy as a solution to their financial problems. To many, what is legally right is morally right and individual bankruptcy is not a disgrace but just smart business tactics.[11]

From a biblical perspective, is there stigma attached to bankruptcy? Is the declaration of bankruptcy unethical? If so, how should a bankrupt Christian be treated? Is he or she a candidate for church discipline? Must bankrupt Christians labor, for the rest of life if necessary, to repay creditors they have "bilked"? We turn now to possible answers.

Chapter 2
The Emotional and Spiritual Impact of Bankruptcy

I don't recommend it. But go through it, and, if you are successful, you can look back with a lot of satisfaction.
—John Ziegler, successful businessman who went through a bankruptcy

The Rotary Club meeting at which I was guest speaker concluded with my address. I had spoken on the emotional impact of bankruptcy. As I gathered my notes, one club member told me he had not only enjoyed the remarks but also identified with much of what I had said.

I told him of a conference where I had given a similar speech and been approached afterward by a former contractor. He was a big, burly individual, but as he shared his personal experience with bankruptcy, and especially the way the church had treated him as a result, he broke down and cried.

"Yes," said my Rotarian friend, softly. "I identify with that, too."

For many, many thousands of participants in business life, prosperity, security, and a positive self-image are just words in a dictionary. One only has to think of the widespread drought of 1988 and its terrible impact on farmers to realize how tenuous security can be. Many people going through the devastating effects of bankruptcy have turned to the church for help, only to be met either by rebuffs or ignorance of bankruptcy's pain.

The origin of this chapter is an article on the emotional and spiritual impact of bankruptcy which I co-wrote with my good friend Ron Toews, a Christian family counselor. He has kindly given me permission to include his material in this book. I extend my grateful thanks to Ron.

My purpose here is to help church leaders and counselors understand how bankruptcy and business failure can hurt the emotional and spiritual well-being of Christians. Perhaps such understanding can help churches become places of healing for Christians wounded by financial trouble.

His name is Bernard. He arrived in Canada from Europe in the 1960s to "pursue the American dream"—a desire born of his upbringing in a low-income family. For several years he was increasingly successful in business. This led to corresponding increases in income, a sense of well-being, and a feeling of self-confidence. A separation from his wife was the only shadow in an otherwise bright picture.

Then a move from industry to a partnership with a cousin whom he learned was an alcoholic brought the dream crashing down. Recession rocked their business. Money drained away. His cousin misused his power-of-attorney to seize total control of the company's remaining assets.

As Bernard later recalled, all his idols—money, success, the dream of being a self-made man, his relationships with his cousin and with a girlfriend on whom he had become very dependent—collapsed. He was virtually penniless, unemployed, his credit exhausted. Yet he still had alimony and a five-figure bank loan to pay. In the winter of 1981 he huddled for warmth in a camper (his only remaining asset) in a parking lot.

At about this time Bernard became a Christian. Through an incredible series of events he realized an almost immediate financial turnaround. By the end of the year he was out of debt and in a position to invest in a significant business. But this venture again met with failure. Once more Bernard was bankrupt. A professional man, he was forced to earn a small income as a part-time entertainer. Only recently has he secured professional employment again.

I asked Bernard how he viewed his experiences with business failure from a Christian perspective. Did he feel that he now carried a stigma, that God was judging him for moral and spiritual mistakes?

Not at all. Rather than assessing his failures as judgment from God, he saw them as direction. "My faith was never shaken," he claimed, "and my self-image is intact. God did everything he could to prove to me that I could trust him."

Among other things, Bernard has found that he can be content in all circumstances. Money and career are no longer his idols. Now he is using his experiences to support others enduring the desperation of business failure.

Bernard's story is amazing and perhaps inspiring, but his reaction to bankruptcy and unemployment is not typical, even for Christians. Studies indicate that most adult males in North America get their feelings of self-worth from their jobs. Without employment, one's self-worth is affected.

This was certainly the experience of Tom. A Christian businessman with an excellent track record, his investments unexpectedly turned sour, leaving him unemployed. Unlike Bernard, Tom saw the experience as one of desolation. An acute sense of failure led Tom to see himself as having no worth. He found he was unable to pray. Not knowing where to turn, he became increasingly depressed. More than anything else, he needed someone to lean on, someone who had "been there."

In our conversation he noted that much bankruptcy protection is available—but there are few resources to help in rebuilding one's personal life. Church people who want to be resource persons for hurting Christians must understand the emotional and spiritual impact of bankruptcy.

There are two influences which have a profound effect on the *emotional* impact of bankruptcy. One is the sources of an individual's self-esteem. The other is the individual's level of involvement in the business which has failed. The *spiritual* impact is often a function of the connection seen between right standing before God and business success.

Emotional impact

Pivotal to a Christian's self-esteem is the recognition that she or he has value as a creature made in God's image. This realization places one's value beyond the standard of personal accomplishment. Further, a network of effective relationships should grow out of this nucleus of a self-worth rooted in God's image. God has made persons to be relational, interdependent, and responsive to one another. An intact nucleus surrounded by a hub of relationships creates a stable sense of self-esteem.

Preston Manning was for many years a Christian business consultant and conference speaker from Edmonton, Alberta. He has had many opportunities to witness people's reactions to business failure. He outlines a typical scenario. Financially stressed people search desperately for money, doing things they would reject under normal circumstances. Family homes may be mortgaged and friends and relatives approached about loans.

Thus, if their businesses go under, their entire family and social structures are affected. They are increasingly isolated and lonely. Their pride in their entrepreneurial abilities leads them to conceal difficulties, particularly from other business people. In fact, they will cut off communication to avoid the awful question, "How are things going?"

Meanwhile their self-image, rooted in accomplishment and not buttressed by healthy and supportive relationships, deteriorates. At one time they saw themselves as indepen-

dent, self-reliant, enterprising. Now they find themselves at
the mercy of their creditors.

Often overlooked is the fact that businesses are far more
than centers of economic activity for many owners. Manning tells of the family farm which could often be liquidated
and the assets put in government savings bonds at a better
rate of return—without the work! But for many owners,
business is a style of life embodying dreams and hopes. If
the business gets sick, the entrepreneur may fall ill as
well—physically, emotionally, spiritually.[1]

> Eric Wall has been a berry grower for 21 years, and this is the
> first year he has pulled out healthy raspberry plants. He didn't
> like it, but he thinks if other growers plowed under some of their
> berries, they could get back some control of the industry again.
> "Yesterday morning this was a berry field just like the others.
> When I plowed them out I almost cried," he said.[2]

Self-esteem is a fragile commodity. It is strongly affected
by one's personal accomplishment plus the status success
buys. Bankruptcy usually devastates these two components.
If they have been substituted for the more biblical foundation of self-esteem discussed above, bankruptcy will quickly
destroy the individual's emotional well-being. The "self-
made man" (or, increasingly, woman) who stands alone, ne-
glecting intimate personal relationships is more likely to be
heavily shaken when bankruptcy occurs.

As mentioned earlier, the emotional pain of bankruptcy
varies with the level of involvement in the business. For
many business people, the business is a total lifestyle involvement which incorporates personal habits and possibly
family history.

Some may not be quite as absorbed but still receive their
sole income from the company, as well as much status. Others attach little status to their business involvements, seeing
them only as an income source. A bankruptcy in this situa-

tion simply eliminates the main source of revenue.

Emotional pain will vary as well with the owner's expectations concerning the company's stability. At one end of the spectrum is a well-established business seen as a permanent fixture. When this business fails, it surprises not only persons closely involved with it, but also the broader community as well. Such failure typically carries with it high emotional pain.

> I had never heard of Chapter 11, and I had had no experience with bankruptcy. But in 1957, after years of building thousands of boats, we had 228 creditors to whom we owed half-a-million dollars, and we had no money to pay them. . . . During those years on the edge of bankruptcy, I felt as if I were sitting in the ashes with Job.[3]

At the other end of the continuum is the business struggling to become established. Statistics suggest that the majority of new small businesses fail in a few years. The emotional impact of bankruptcy in these cases is usually much lower.

Spiritual impact

The spiritual impact may be acute if the businessperson has been influenced by the "gospel of prosperity" doctrine. Labeled as everything from a heresy or a cult to part of the full gospel, this success theology links material prosperity and business success with divine favor and right standing before God.

Its cruder expression is nicely captured in the following segment of a sermon given by Bob Harrington, the famed chaplain of Bourbon Street in New Orleans.

> Money—when you have more of it you can pray better, you can shout better, you can sing better, you can build schools better, you can build bigger churches better; so don't you think just because you happen to be succeeding dollarwise that that makes you not right with God!. . . .

Successful and saved—same thing! You can't be saved without wanting to be successful, because that's God's plan for you and for me.

Richard De Vos, cofounder of Amway, expresses similar sentiments.

Somehow it always struck me in the Old Testament that some of God's greatest heroes were the richest guys in town. . . . Obviously God wasn't hung up on some guy who was rich. I think if you go through a whole lot of the Old Testament and some of the New, you'll perceive that he *promises* you riches. "I'll give you more than you can ever imagine if you keep me first and work as I would have you work."[4]

When Christian businesspeople who have been exposed to such teaching go bankrupt, they may conclude there is something wrong with their relationship with God. If poverty is outside of God's intended will, then they must be leading a Satan-defeated life. Rather than resting in God's providential care, they feel condemned.

Where does the doctrine of success religion come from? Gordon D. Fee, Professor of New Testament at Regent College in Vancouver, British Columbia, and an Assemblies of God minister, points out that a frequently cited text is 3 John 2, which in the King James Version says, "Beloved, I wish above all things that thou mayest prosper and be in health even as thy soul prospereth."

One gospel of wealth proponent suggests that John means Christians should prosper *materially.* Fee shows, however, that the word *prosper* means simply "to go well with someone." It was the standard form of greeting in a personal letter. He adds,

To extend John's greeting to Gaius to refer to financial and material prosperity for all Christians of all times is totally foreign to the text. One might as well argue that all Christians with sick stomachs are not to pray for healing or go to the doctor but rather to stop drinking water and start drinking wine instead (1 Tim. 5:23).

Fee cites another commonly misused text, John 10:10: "I have come that they may have life, and have it abundantly" (or, to the full). No allusion to material abundance is meant here, either. Fee maintains that the word *life* in John's Gospel is the equivalent of "the kingdom of God" in the Synoptics. It literally means "the life in the age to come."

This life is God's gift to believers in the present age. Christians are to enjoy this gift "to the full." Material abundance is not implied either in the word "life" or in the phrase "to the full."[5]

Paul, in Philippians 4:11, tells us that he is *content* in all circumstances. He employs the Greek word *autarkes*, an important quality describing a person's independence of things. This kind of contentment was a self-sufficiency taught by the Stoics. The philosopher Seneca, for instance, maintained that "the happy man is content [*autarkes*] with his present lot, no matter what it is, and is reconciled to his circumstances."

The Stoic self-sufficient person faced life with resources found within, whereas Paul found the secret of his contentment in his union with Christ. But Paul shared with the Stoics their disregard for material circumstances. Thus in 1 Timothy 6 he tells those who have nothing to be content with food and clothing. The rich are to treat their wealth as an opportunity to meet the needs of others. For neither rich nor poor was wealth a measure of relationship with God.

Success stories
as in business
as in industry
as in academic life.

Success: the criterion
by which we measure ourselves
and others.

Making it (breaking others).
Sitting on top (looking down).
Comparing (being better).

How strange a success,
that of Christ dying on the cross.
    —Ulrich Schaffer[6]

Businesspeople who have not been directly influenced by
the gospel of wealth may still conclude that failure results
from being out of God's favor. This is especially so if they
see human suffering as coming only from God's judgment.

Several bankrupt businesspeople I interviewed had a
very different perspective, however. Their suffering was
more like Job's. Bankruptcy left them frustrated and con-
fused. They felt their business practices were aboveboard.
Their risk-taking was appropriate, given the circumstances.

Typically, they received much moral support from Christian brothers and sisters during their business crisis. They
concluded that through their time of failure they learned to
depend on God rather than business acumen. But they interpreted God's dealings with them as *teaching,* not judgment.

This is not to deny that God might judge the way an individual handles business or personal affairs. Some
"Christian" businesspeople have been guilty of shocking
business behavior. Such people are candidates for church
discipline. But unless one sees bankruptcy as inherently
sinful, one will agree that many individuals who have declared bankruptcy should be offered support and counsel,
not rejection.

Meeting the spiritual and emotional needs

How, then, can church leaders best meet the needs of
Christians facing business or personal bankruptcy? Preston
Manning feels strongly that God's providential care of indi-

viduals must be stressed. He does not necessarily believe that God will rescue businesses from financial trouble. Rather, Manning concludes that God is in the business of saving persons from such circumstances.

> Where God intervenes in human affairs, the focus in the Bible is on saving persons—not gardens, land, armies, vineyards, kingdoms, ships, towers, governments, businesses, churches, political parties, enterprises, schools or programs, but persons. One's reaction might be, "I don't need saving, it's the business that needs saving. I'd gladly sacrifice myself if God would save my business." But Scripture seems to say that it is *you, the innermost you . . . the soul and spirit of you* that God is first and foremost interested in saving, rescuing, preserving, sustaining. . . . Sometimes God has also been known to save a few gardens, armies, kingdoms, ships, churches, careers and businesses, but his focus is on *you*.[7]

Manning calls for churches and Christian organizations to establish small groups of Christian laypeople to minister to bankrupts and others in financial trouble. The group would ideally be composed of people who have been through similar circumstances and know something about the ministry of comfort grounded in God's providential care.

Milt Kuyers is president of a manufacturing company in Milwaukee, Wisconsin. He writes concerning a unique employment program in his hometown.

> Christian businesspersons from my church are working with an inner-city church, Lighthouse Gospel Church, which in the recent past had an extremely high level of unemployment. Lighthouse's pastor, James Carrington; Lighthouse's members; and Christian businesspersons from Brookfield Christian Reformed Church work together to provide the individual support necessary to keep frequently unemployed people employed.
>
> Together we have touched the lives of thirty-five people in the past one-and-a-half years. Because of this program, Lighthouse, a church of 250 members, has gone from 20 percent unemployment to full employment.

The success of the program has not come easily, however. Pastor Carrington spends many hours counseling the workers from his church, encouraging them to persevere when they feel like quitting. His church and ministry help those members of his congregation who cannot lean on a solid family tradition of employment.

We business owners, in turn, make special efforts to work through potential problems with our Lighthouse workers. We also deal with criticism of these efforts from within our own companies. At times we have daily contact with Pastor Carrington to discuss how we can both help with a worker's personal problem. This close relationship has averted potential crises.[8]

Manning's position is also strongly endorsed by Tom (mentioned earlier). Tom's greatest need during his year of unemployment and self-doubt was for someone who could empathize with his plight. Such a person would supply both spiritual counseling and a logical, experienced mind.

First, this helper would provide "an anchor in decision-making," keeping his friend from making ill-advised choices. Tom compared his experience of unemployment to the grieving process. Filled with feelings of shock and anger, he was in no position to make rational decisions.[9] A counselor would help the bankrupt person evaluate what has happened and learn from past mistakes.

Second, the friend would encourage the bankrupt to trust in God's providence and maintain a sense of self-worth.

A broad support network of family, friends, and business peers who remain loyal through the bankruptcy process is vital to the bankrupt. Both the person experiencing loss as well as his or her supporters must be realistic, however. They may naively assume that when the legal work is done the emotional issues will have been resolved. On the contrary, the emotional issues may linger for a long time, perhaps even after new revenue is flowing.

A person experiencing bankruptcy must go through a two-stage process. First, an emotional unhooking from the lost business. Second, personal rebuilding and engagement in another job or business endeavor.

The first stage is not easily achieved in many cases. From the time a person first realizes the business is in trouble until the bankruptcy process ends, he or she may experience tremendous emotional turbulence. Crushed hopes, family tensions, court battles, and feelings of failure and inadequacy can take an almost unimaginable toll.

It is important that the bankrupt be connected to a person who can help the individual deal with these emotions over time. It is also important that the bankrupt avoid deep involvement in another business during this period. However, as the emotional healing comes, the bankrupt can turn from unhooking to the second stage of personal rebuilding. Now past mistakes can teach lessons because emotional issues are not clouding judgment. The bankrupt can assess future potential and begin seriously to pursue permanent career opportunities.

Many individuals who have gone through bankruptcy will attest to both its negative and positive aspects. Bankruptcy lawyer David Gagnon, for instance, cites this testimonial.

> I consider bankruptcy to be a positive process. Although everyone views bankruptcy with dread, it does represent the safety net which preserves debtors from financial calamity . . . [Concerning a couple in their 60's who had once been millionaires but then lost everything when their business failed, leaving them with debts they could never repay]: Debtors in those circumstances are desperate, usually broken in spirit, and occasionally suicidal.
>
> Financial rebirth through bankruptcy, even for those in their 60's, can restore the glint in their eyes. They can face the future with dignity again.[10]

Another counselor friend of mine suggested three important bankruptcy lessons. First, it certainly qualifies as one of life's major softening experiences, leaving a person transformed by God to deal far more gently with others.

Second, in rebuilding one's life, an honest and searching evaluation of one's goals, values, skills, and interests is called for. My friend pointed out that the Chinese ideogram for *crisis* is apparently composed of two other ideograms representing *danger* and *opportunity*. The bankrupt may realize that a change to another line of work could bring new joy.

Third, bankruptcy is an opportunity to cut oneself loose from overdependence on material wealth.

We now come to one last practical point raised by Tom. He mentioned the need for a friend who would not only stabilize and build up the person coping with business failure—but also "dare to risk with you again."

There are individuals and even churches prepared to offer a Christian sister or brother financial help to make a fresh start. Whether offered funds are treated as debt, equity, or an outright gift will vary, of course, with individual cases.

But the operative principle is surely stated in James 2:15-17: If one of the brothers or one of the sisters is in need of clothes and has not enough food to live on, and one of you says to them, "I wish you well; keep yourself warm and eat plenty, without giving them these bare necessities of life, then what good is that? Faith is like that: if good works do not go with it, it is quite dead" (JB).

PART 2
Bankruptcy: Where It Came from and How It Works

After six years of bankruptcy, the creditors agreed to forgive 80% of the money we had lost for them. Then about 1965 God began to prosper the business.

We have learned to tithe the profits. We take what God sends in and each year write a check for 10% of it, which is over the 5% the government allows as a write-off for charitable purposes.

I was speaking on a Christian college campus and a student asked me afterward, "Mr. Meloon, should I tithe? Did you tithe when you owed so much money?"

"Yes, sir!" I responded.

"You mean that when you owe money to other people you should still tithe?"

"If people don't give to God's work until they have their home and car paid for, God would never get anything! God tells us to give our tithes and gifts to him, and he promises to supply all our needs." And he does.

We were in debt $1 million. We have been systematically

paying back every dollar—including the 80% that our creditors forgave.

Every payment goes out with a letter that says, "Because of what Jesus Christ has done for us, we're able to pay you what you lost with us 20 years ago."

And you should see the letters we get in return! I know now why I had 228 creditors: God wanted me to be able to witness to 228 people!

Walter O. Meloon, "I had 228 Creditors," *Power for Living*, July 3, 1983. Originally published in *Alliance Life* (formerly *The Alliance Witness*) May 16, 1979. Used by permission.

Chapter 3
The Major Causes of Bankruptcy

In my business, 'tis true that strength and bustle build
up a firm. But judgment and knowledge are what keep it
established. Unluckily, I am bad at science, Farfrae; bad
at figures—a rule o'thumb sort of man.
　　　　—The Mayor of Casterbridge, Thomas Hardy

Business Bankruptcies

At the height of the recession in the early eighties, it was assumed that the large number of commercial failures could be traced to the high rates of interest dampening economic activity.

Consider the following headline, however. "Business Failures Worst in 40 Years." The date was—1972, when interest rates were around 5%. A 1976 headline declared, "Bankruptcies Up 33%—Worse Ahead." Interest rates at that time were about 8%.[1]

Economic observers are more apt to view interest rates as a catalyst to failure than a cause. While many reasons are given for bankruptcy, three in particular stand out.

Poor management

Dun and Bradstreet cite the following reasons for business failure:

62.1%—Incompetence
16.4%—Lack of managerial experience

10.0%—Lack of experience in the line of business
9.1%—Lack of scope in expertise
2.4%—Miscellaneous factors such as fraud or bad luck.[2]

Other studies have arrived at similar conclusions concerning the devastating effects of inadequate management. According to a European survey, for instance, managerial shortcomings were responsible for over 65% of all business bankruptcies.[3]

Larry Greiner, in an article entitled "Evolution and Revolution as Organizations Grow,"[4] points out that in the beginning stages the founders of a business concentrate on creating a product and a market. They are usually technically or entrepreneurially inclined. They have little interest in management activities.

These new businesses characteristically include frequent and informal communication among employees, long hours of work accompanied by modest salaries, and control of activities coming from immediate marketplace feedback—management acts as the customers react.

Such characteristics are vital to getting a new company going. But they are inadequate when the business grows. As manufacturing becomes more complex, the number of employees increases, or more sophisticated controls are necessary, the entrepreneur shrinks from unwanted management responsibilities. Fundamentally new requirements for leadership now appear.

At this point many businesses fail. The owners refuse to face their lack of management know-how and experience. They fail to plan—probably the predominant flaw of entrepreneurs. They ignore mundane matters—inventory control, adequate cash flow to pay the bills, or establishing credit and collection policies.[5]

Business magazine editor Tom Messer suggests that during times of economic expansion most small and medium businesses are successful. But only "geniuses" can make ends meet during recessions. Genius, in this case, is ability to foresee environmental changes, or at least capacity to adapt quickly. Owners more inclined to be "doers" than planners tend to adapt to change slowly. They are therefore vulnerable to swings in the business climate.[6]

Some owners do adjust, perhaps by hiring a competent manager or by securing sufficient management education. Organizational structures are overhauled. Communication lines are formalized. Appropriate controls are put in place. More competent direction is given.

Once again, however, growth places new demands on leadership. Lower-level employees, finding themselves restricted by the hierarchy, feel shut out of decisions, despite their expert knowledge. Growing disenchanted, valuable employees often leave.

Turnover rate among key employees is an indication of management quality. A common forerunner of business failure is one-man rule. The owner fails to consult employees or other resource people. He refuses to delegate responsibility and appropriate authority to employees who have developed certain kinds of expertise. Understandably, capable employees leave.

Another form of poor management frequently observed is refusal to take advantage of resource persons outside the firm. Yet such help is available. For example, Canada's Federal Business Development Bank has organized CASE, or Counseling Assistance to Small Enterprises, staffed by some two thousand retired business people. For a fraction of a consultant's fee, the wisdom of years of business success can be made available to struggling firms.

Undercapitalization and overtrade

The Financial Post Magazine reports that whereas in the 1960s banks provided 17% of corporate funds, by the 1970s this figure had reached 50%. Entrepreneurs have been increasingly reluctant to put up their own money. But bank financing represents fixed overhead. This lacks the flexibility of equity financing. While owners can defer dividends in hard times, the bank comes calling every month.[7]

Many owners, of course, simply start out without enough money. They have nothing to fall back on when times turn tough. Their last dime is in the business.

In addition, many entrepreneurs, valuing their independence, refuse to consider finding a private investor who could inject money into the business and reduce dependence on lending institutions.

The situation is often complicated by what is called overtrading. The owners increase sales and assets at a greater rate than they can sustain. For instance, the plant may be expanded to meet increased demand, but the cash flow does not cover the increased expenses. Their working capital is insufficient to meet the demand.[8]

Lack of adequate financial information

"An inadequate financial reporting system," says Rea Godbold, "is probably the biggest single fault we find as receivers. The company has no idea what it costs to make or market its product and consequently no strategy for adapting to changing conditions."[9]

Many analysts cite poor recordkeeping as the critical cause of failure. *The Financial Times* notes the following serious but common errors.[10]

a. Little or no financial planning and only rudimentary reporting systems. A company may be in a poor shape and not realize its condition until the point of no return.
b. Lax control of accounts receivable and payable. Naturally, in tough times no one is in a hurry to pay his bills. Some companies have used a discount policy as an incentive to prompt payment. Careful attention to payables is essential to retaining good credit status.

c. Sloppy inventory analysis. Many small businesses are chronically short of funds, often because they tie up money in borderline products and services.
d. Cost control that doesn't go far enough. This extends from the deferral of capital equipment expenditures to cutbacks in one's personal lifestyle, a sacrifice which poses difficulties for some entrepreneurs according to a management consultant.

> "The real problem comes when the drastic steps that are necessary become visible to the community. When I must tell him he has to drive a Pontiac instead of a Cadillac, and that his wife is not going to drive a Lincoln, his self-esteem is hit. He cannot accept that he's no longer the big spender at the club, and that he won't have 50 football tickets to give away every weekend. It really is sad, because all this is part of the way many people have built their businesses."[11]

e. Poor communications with bankers and other creditors. The following quote from a trustee in bankruptcy I interviewed is representative of the conviction of most experts:

> "The last thing a creditor wants is for a borrower to go bankrupt, as the likelihood of recovering the debt is low. Provided the borrower is open, honest, and is dialoguing with the creditor, the latter will make remarkable accommodations to keep the borrower afloat."

Fortunately, modern technology has placed timely financial information well within the reach of even the smallest firms through inexpensive computer hardware and software. "Straight bookkeeping is the least of your concerns," maintains one author. "Why pay some $1000 a month just to keep your books when you can get it all put on a computer for $50."[12]

While the above three causes of bankruptcy are mentioned most often, there are others which frequently help cause business failure. More than one bank loans officer interviewed was prepared to blame his own institution. One study of small business failures revealed that in 87% of the cases examined, the bank was the instigator of bankruptcy action, and rarely was the bank not fully covered with client collateral.[13]

Another loans officer told me that banks became too liberal in lending because of intense competition. Another suggested that many bankers are poorly trained and do not counsel owner/borrowers properly. The controversial Canadian Farmers Survival Association maintained that banks are not willing to take any risk. Banks, they say, prefer to let the farmer shoulder that burden alone. Banks show no compassion during difficult times, even if the farmer is open and honest with the bank.[14]

Occasionally bankruptcies are the result of corrupt practices, either by the businessperson or by someone with whom the business deals. In a previous chapter I introduced Walter Meloon, the Christian businessman whose boat-building company faced bankruptcy. Here is his explanation of how it happened.

Shortly before this [running out of money to pay creditors], the chief government inspector on a contract for 3,000 fiberglass boats we were building for the Corps of Engineers had asked us to pay him and the other inspectors by taking care of their hotel rooms and meals. We knew that the government also paid for their rooms and meals. We had built 36,000 boats for the government during World War II and the Korean War, and we had never been approached by anyone else to take care of their expenses. My brother and I discussed the request and we decided that we should forget about it.

The inspector did not forget. We soon had 600 boats that failed to meet his specifications. He told our bankers that he was not accepting our boats and that they had better withdraw their funds. At times we thought, "Why not pay the man off? It isn't much compared to what the company stands to lose."

It wasn't the money but something far deeper. At night I'd lie awake wrestling with the problem. One night, trying not to disturb my wife, I slipped out of bed and knelt on the living room floor with an open Bible on the stool in front of me. In the light of my lamp these words seemed to glow: "Trust in the Lord with all thine heart; and lean not unto thine own understanding. In all thy ways acknowledge him, and he shall direct thy paths."

I thought, "That has to be our answer. To pay off the man would not be trusting the Lord, but rather giving in to the devious ways of the world."

Then came the final blow! A flat-car had just been loaded with 40 "approved" boats when the chief inspector suddenly appeared and said, "I don't like their looks. They've got to be unloaded and refinished."

That arbitrary decision made it impossible for us to continue. The contract had already cost the company one million dollars, and we owed half-a-million to our creditors.[15]

Another all-too-common reason for bankruptcy involves con artists who buy legitimate companies with long-established credit records and then bankrupt them. Financial writer John Haskett outlines a typical scam.

Large quantities of easily-disposable merchandise are purchased. The suppliers should tumble to the plan, as orders usually far exceed normal requirements, and are often for completely unrelated products—a wholesale plumbing firm, for example, will start to buy large amounts of expensive office equipment, far in excess of normal needs—but too often the desire for a sale clouds their judgments.

Then the scam operators start to unload the excess merchandise, often through channels expressly set up for the rapid movement of such "hot" goods. The money is put into the company coffers but soon withdrawn, to pay off shareholders' loans and other fictitious claims.

By the time the creditors start getting nervous the con men have drained the company of all assets. When the first hearing rolls around all that's left is a shell, and creditors are lucky to salvage a dime on the dollar.[16]

Most often, however, the fault lies primarily with the borrowers, not the lenders. Many business people develop sloppy habits in affluent times. Then they do not change when business conditions demand a more tightly run ship.

Market factors pose another critical problem. Some companies become too dependent on one or a few customers. Or they provide a product prone to dramatic change. In addition, some business people will jump into an expensive new venture without first doing a proper market assessment and developing an appropriate marketing plan.

Owning a business is risky. It is estimated that about 300,000 new companies are formed in the United States each year. About two-thirds of them fail within five years. Management is consistently cited as the key to success. But the dismal record of business failure only proves the telling statement, "Few businesses plan to fail but most small businesses fail to plan."

Personal Bankruptcies

A comprehensive study of personal or consumer bankrupts published in 1982 indicates that the main cause of personal bankruptcies in Canada is mismanaged or excessive consumer debt.[17] This is not surprising to anyone who is aware of the explosion of consumer debt in North America. *Time Magazine* reports:

> Nobody advocates a strictly cash economy, of course, but in a country that once admired Ben Franklin's rule that it was better to "go to bed supperless than run in debt for breakfast," the accumulation of personal debt is staggering. Installment credit grew last year (i.e., 1981) by a total of $20 billion, to $333 billion. . . . Adding home mortgages, the total is more than $1.5 trillion. Personal debt averages out to $6,737 for every American. And more and more often people cannot pay: personal bankruptcies, 179,194 in 1978, reached 456,914 last year.[18]

Canadian figures also indicate an increasing use of credit purchasing. Consumer credit outstanding (exclusive of home mortgages and business debt) reached about $50 billion in 1985. Dividing this by Canada's population yields consumer credit outstanding per capita of approximately

$2000. In 1970 Canadians' credit purchases were about $600 per capita. Even with adjustments for inflation, the increased use of credit is considerable. For instance, between 1950 and 1985, the per capita increase was more than five times using constant dollars.[19]

The analysis of consumer bankrupts done by Consumer and Corporate Affairs Canada reveals disturbing data. First, consumer bankrupts tend to be younger than the adult population at large. About 63% of these bankrupts were under age 35, a disproportionate number as only 43% of Canadians generally fall into this age category. Only 8% of consumer bankrupts were age fifty or more.[20]

Second, a disproportionate number of personal bankrupts lack employable skills. Managerial and professional people represent 9.8% of the Canadian labor force but only 2.9% of consumer bankrupts.

The addition of semiprofessionals, middle managers, foremen, and technicians brings the total to 27.6% of the labor force but only 14% of bankrupts. People employed in various skilled and semiskilled occupations such as crafts and trades, sales, clerical work, and so on are proportionately represented: 49% of the labor force and 47.7% of consumer bankrupts.

The last category is particularly unsettling. Unskilled clerical, sales, and service personnel and unskilled manual labor constitute 23.4% of employed people—but a whopping 38.8% of those who declared personal bankruptcy.[21]

Consumer bankrupts are drawn heavily from the lowest skill levels. As might be expected, given this data, the incomes of consumer bankrupts are generally quite low.[22]

Approximately 49% of these people gave consumer debt as their reason for bankruptcy. A breakdown of their creditors is rather interesting.

1. Finance and acceptance companies. 74% owed these institutions at least one debt and 37% had two or more such debts.

2. Chartered banks. 61% of consumer bankrupts had one bank loan and 24% two or more.
3. Department stores were owed by 46% and other retailers by 41%.
4. Bank credit cards. Perhaps surprisingly, considering their ease of use, only about 30% of bankrupts reported money owing on these well-known cards.
5. Credit unions had much less trouble with borrowers. Only 21% reported owing money to this source.
6. Other sources of consumer credit included gas and other credit cards, medical and dental bills, and collection agency or credit bureau bills. These were reported by about 17% or less of those surveyed.[23]

A number of questions come to mind. Why do lending institutions provide credit so freely to people with lower-skilled, low-income jobs? Additionally, what prompts so many younger people with a lack of good occupational and financial prospects to burden themselves with consumer debt? The median indebtedness of those in the study was $10,865, while median assets were about $400.[24]

In response to the second question, a trustee who specializes in personal bankruptcies says that

> Bankruptcy is very much an attitudinal thing, a commitment to one's obligations. It takes very little to be technically in a situation of going bankrupt—debts of more than $1000 and the inability to pay. Many use bankruptcy as a tool to avoid paying debts, especially younger people who believe that they have the right to a certain standard of living without putting out for it. They are unwilling to sacrifice to meet financial obligations. And until recently credit institutions have supported such attitudes with liberal credit policies.

In addition to consumer debt, reasons given for personal bankruptcy included unemployment (15%), operations of, or guarantees for, a business (14%), health and misfortune (14%), and marital and family problems (7%).[25]

The American experience is very similar. Bankruptcy

experts cite easy credit from credit card companies, marital problems, alcohol or drug abuse, cut in pay, lost job, rising interest rates on adjustable-rate mortgages, and unexpected medical expenses as the chief causes of bankruptcy filings.

The authors of the excellent Consumer and Corporate Affairs study tried to find at least partial solutions to an increasingly worrisome phenomenon. First, they note that many bankrupts seemed unaware of the precariousness of their financial situation until legal action was threatened or taken. Few had previously sought debt counseling. The authors recommend debt counseling at critical times. They also advise more teaching of money management skills in school.

In addition, they see the credit-granting industry as bearing much of the blame. "In short, getting further credit was too easy. There is a responsibility for credit grantors, especially cash lenders, to participate in joint industry, government, and voluntary sector efforts to detect and help avert impending consumer insolvencies requiring bankruptcy as a solution."[26]

Chapter 4
The Bankruptcy Process and Its Alternatives

Going bankrupt might provide financial and emotional relief. But going through the process could be stressful.
    —Mike Grenby, financial columnist

Relationships between creditors and lenders have always been filled with tension, hostility, suspicion, evasion, turmoil, exploitation—even death. Over the centuries societies have attempted to regulate these relationships so that creditors' claims are protected—while debtors are also protected when circumstances warrant.

The History of Bankruptcy

In ancient times, the security demanded for a loan was often the debtor. This personal security might extend to the debtor's family and all possessions. Thus, if the debtor failed to repay, debtor and family often had to enter into the exclusive service of the creditor until the debt was discharged.

In fifth century B.C. Rome, for instance, a borrower signed a contract called a *nexum*. This allowed the lender to seize the person of the borrower, without judgment, for defaulting on the loan. Defaulters often were sold abroad into slavery or even put to death by the creditors.[1]

Enlightened rulers tried to alleviate the worst abuses. Hammurabi (c. 1750 B.C.), in his famous Code, allowed creditors to levy a "distress" or "pledge," called a *niputum*, if the debt was not paid. However, the creditor who wrongfully levied the distress was penalized.[2]

Fourth century B.C. Roman law altered the *nexum*. Before a debtor could be seized, the case had to be brought before a magistrate.[3] Eventually Roman law allowed a distinction between the debtor whose inability to repay was for reasons beyond control and a borrower who obtained credit fraudulently. In the former case, the debtor could avoid enslavement or execution by turning all assets over to the creditor.[4]

An act governing bankruptcy first appeared in Italy in the late Middle Ages. The term *bankruptcy* has an interesting origin. Italian creditors, wishing to show their displeasure that a debtor had failed to meet obligations, would visit the debtor's place of business and smash the workbench. "Broken bench" in Italian is *banca rotta*.

English law dealing with insolvency first appeared in 1351. It provided that if any member of the Company of Lombard Merchants acknowledged being a debtor, the Company must guarantee repayment if the individual merchant defaulted.

This act and others which followed stressed the rights of creditors. Debtors were to surrender all property if bankrupt. Fraudulent debtors were severely punished. In fact, the Act of 1571 restricted bankruptcy to those engaged in trade. An individual not involved in trade, who could not pay off debts, was thrown in prison and kept there until someone else paid them. Not until the 19th century were such debtors allowed to avoid incarceration through surrender of their assets to their creditors.[5]

The current Canadian bankruptcy legislation, which allows for a joint court/creditor control of bankruptcy proceedings, is patterned somewhat on the English Bankruptcy Act of 1883. Its purposes can be noted from the following summary of an address made by the then President of the Board of Trade.

He asked the House to keep in mind the two main, and, at the same time, distinct objects of any good Bankruptcy law. Those were, firstly, in the honest administration of bankrupt estates, with a view to the fair and speedy distribution of the assets among the creditors, whose property they were; and in the second place their object should be, following the idea that prevention was better than cure, to do something to improve the general tone of commercial morality, to promote honest trading, and to lessen the number of failures. His next point was that, with regard to those most important objects, there was only one way by which they could be secured and that was by securing an independent and impartial examination into the circumstances of each case.[6]

Canada introduced its first insolvency legislation in 1869. The Bankruptcy Act of 1919 provided for the liquidation of the assets and release from further obligation of the honest debtor. It did not, however, protect the fraudulent debtor.

Current Bankruptcy Law

Changes since have clarified and streamlined proceedings. No major changes have occurred since 1966, although a new act has been in discussion for some time. The U.S. has more recently revised its bankruptcy legislation. It passed the Bankruptcy Reform Act of 1978, with a further revision in 1984.

If a company is experiencing serious financial problems, a number of voluntary alternatives may be available to owners. For instance, if the business continues to be viable, the owners could reorganize, refinance, or make a proposal to their creditors which would result in a better payoff than bankruptcy would provide. If viability is in doubt but the company is still solvent, then statutory liquidation is possible. If the owners face insolvency, they may consider a voluntary bankruptcy.

However, a company may not be able to take advantage of such voluntary initiatives. In Canada, for instance, a secured creditor can send in a receiver to take over a company when the lender is worried about the safety of its collateral. And, of course, one's creditors may petition a firm (or an individual) into involuntary bankruptcy.

Space does not allow discussion of all the above concepts. What follows is an outline of the usual steps in the bankruptcy process in Canada and the United States for companies and individuals. If you will allow a little patriotism, I will overview Canadian bankruptcy law first.

The Bankruptcy Act is administered by a Superintendent of Bankruptcy. His major responsibilities include the appointment and supervision of trustees, who administer bankrupt estates, and the investigation of possible violations of the Act, especially where fraud is suspected.

The Act designates a particular court, usually the highest trial court in each province, as the agency to deal with bankruptcy matters. Each court has official receivers whose duties include accepting and filing assignments, appointing trustee's, and examining debtor conduct.

Let us focus first on involuntary bankruptcy. One or more creditors with claims totaling at least $1,000 may file in court a petition to place a person or company into bankruptcy. The petitioning creditors must prove that the debtor is insolvent, that the debts owed to the petitioning creditors are at least $1,000, and that the debtor has committed what is called an act of bankruptcy. There are ten such activities defined in the Bankruptcy Act. The following five are the most common.

1. Debtors notify creditors that they have suspended or are about to suspend payments;
2. Debtors show creditors a statement of assets and liabilities which indicate insolvency;
3. Debtors fraudulently transfer title of all or any part of their property;
4. Debtors fail to satisfy an execution served upon them by a

sheriff (an execution orders a court official to take a debtor's property to pay a court-decided debt);
5. Debtors cease to meet their liabilities generally as they become due.

If the court is satisfied as to the legitimacy of the petition, and if the debtor consents to or does not oppose the petition, a receiving order is issued declaring the debtor bankrupt.

The receiving order acts as a stay of proceedings against all except secured creditors. Thus unsecured creditors cannot now take any action against the debtor, such as a landlord seizing assets for nonpayment of rent.

It also permits the appointment of a licensed trustee (usually an accountant) to administer the estate of the bankrupt. While a trustee's services may cost as little as $50 for truly desperate individuals, they are likely to cost much more, often several thousands of dollars, depending on the complexity of the case.

The trustee has the right to obtain all books, records and assets of the bankrupt and to carry out a full investigation of the bankrupt's affairs. One of the trustee's first steps is to call a meeting of the bankrupt's creditors, at which time his or her appointment as trustee is confirmed by the creditors or a substitution is made.

At this meeting the creditors appoint a maximum of five inspectors who supervise the trustee's activities on behalf of the creditors. The main responsibility of the trustee, then, is to collect the estate of the debtor. The purpose is to convert it into cash and to distribute the proceeds to the creditors according to a legislated "pecking order," unsecured creditors coming last. The trustee must follow the directions of the creditors, provided those instructions are not contrary to the Bankruptcy Act.

A bankrupt debtor found to have acted fraudulently (such as by falsifying information given to the trustee) is punished. Penalties can include fine, imprisonment, or having fraudulent transfers of property declared null and void so such property is available for execution by creditors.

However, if no fraud is established, the bankrupt may apply to the court for a discharge from debt obligations. The court has a wide discretion here. For instance, it can impose conditions such as paying certain amounts to creditors, or it can deny a discharge entirely. But the honest (although unfortunate or incompetent) bankrupt will normally be released from all claims of creditors, with certain exceptions such as alimony payments and court fines.

A bankrupt is not released from debts until discharged by the court. Thus any income the bankrupt receives before discharge may be used to pay creditors if the court so decides. In addition, the bankrupt may not engage in any business without disclosing undischarged bankrupt status, nor become a director of a limited liability corporation. The bankrupt cannot purchase goods on credit except for personal necessities (food, for instance).

Voluntary bankruptcy proceedings differ little. An insolvent debtor may file with the official receiver the assignment of property for the general benefit of creditors. The receiver selects a trustee to accept the property and the trustee calls a meeting of the creditors. The vast majority of personal bankruptcies are voluntary.

If a debtor objects to a creditor's petition, the matter goes before a judge. The debtor may then attempt to prove he or she is not bankrupt. If successful, the judge will dismiss the petition.[7]

Two alternatives to bankruptcy are particularly important to the discussion which follows in Chapter 8. The first, an orderly payment of debts (OPD), is applicable to an individual seeking to avoid personal bankruptcy.

Under OPD, a qualifying debtor may obtain a court order which allows consolidation of eligible debts. The consolidation order also substantially limits the action creditors can take against the debtor. Full payment of the debts will normally be made within three years by means of one periodic payment at a reduced rate of interest.[8]

The second alternative, the proposal, is available to both individuals and businesses facing bankruptcy. The proposal is a plan the debtor submits to creditors for paying some or all debts. To be successful, it must obviously offer a better return to creditors than if the company went bankrupt.

The process is as follows. The bankruptcy trustee works with the debtor, and usually the debtor's lawyer or accountant, to draft a proposal they feel is attractive to the creditors. The proposal is deposited with the official receiver.

The trustee then notifies the creditors of a meeting to consider the proposal. Before the meeting, the trustee will probably sound out the secured creditors, who are in a position to seize their security and undermine the whole process, to avoid unexpected opposition.

Within about three weeks the parties meet again and the creditors vote on the proposal. It passes if those in favor constitute 75% of the total debt, and 50% of the total number of creditors.

If the creditors accept the offer, the trustees and debtor appear in bankruptcy court. If the judge also approves the proposal, it becomes binding on all parties. Should either the creditors or the judge reject the proposal, the individual or company automatically goes into bankruptcy.

An example of a fairly elaborate proposal is provided by what was once British Columbia oldest daily newspaper, the *New Westminster Columbian*. The *Columbian's* debts at the time (May 1983) were $7.3 million. The paper's net deficit was another $2.07 million. Its proposal included the following provisions:

1. An offer to its 209 employees to buy up to 25% of the company's stock;

2. The repayment of its 500 unsecured creditors at the rate of
    16 2/3 cents to the dollar annually for three years;
3. The requirement that its trade creditors provide within a
    month up to another $275,000 of credit, repayable on a nor-
    mal 30-day term.

The success rate of proposals, according to a senior official
with the Superintendent of Bankruptcy, is between 70 and
80%. However, comparatively few proposals are ever made
(in 1989, only 570 proposals were filed in Canada).

A number of reasons for this low number are suggested.
First, many debtors do not realize until too late that something must be done. Second, some creditors, as a matter of
principle, may reject a proposal even though they stand to
gain over the debtor going bankrupt. They do not want to
set a precedent of being easy in matters of credit. Third,
bankruptcy offers an individual the most relief from debt,
with little stigma attached in many cases. Thus the incentive
to make a proposal is minimized.

It is unfortunate that more debtors do not take advantage
of the proposal route. Some consultants feel that one-half of
potential bankrupts could turn around their affairs using
this method.[9]

A number of changes to the Bankruptcy Act were being
seriously considered by the federal government at the time
of writing. These include:

1. Helping insolvent companies work themselves out of their
    problems by requiring that the secured creditors (typically
    the bank) give a company ten days' notice that it is going to
    claim assets or appoint a receiver. During the ten days the
    company could put forward a proposal for reorganizing its
    affairs. It would then have thirty days to put together the
    plan. Creditors would have twenty-one days to accept it by a
    two-thirds majority of each class of creditor.
2. Providing greater protection to employees of failed firms.
    The proposed plan would guarantee that workers would re-
    ceive unpaid wages to a maximum of $2,000. They would

also be entitled to receive unpaid expenses up to $1,000. Under the current law employees can claim just $500, and only if money is left over once secured creditors have been paid.

3. Automatically discharging a bankrupt individual from his/her debts after nine months unless a creditor files a formal objection.

American legislation is similar. The Bankruptcy Code consists of eight odd-numbered chapters. Chapters 1, 3, and 5 are general administrative provisions which apply to all bankruptcy proceedings. Chapters 9 and 15 are of a specialized nature and are of no consequence to this overview. This leaves the following.

Chapter 7—*Liquidation*, also known as straight or ordinary bankruptcy.

Chapter 11—*Reorganization*, which provides for reorganization of businesses.

Chapter 13—*Adjustment of Debts of an Individual with Regular Income*, which parallels Canada's Orderly Payment of Debts in many respects.

The bankruptcy proceedings are like the Canadian ones in several respects. A brief overview follows.

1. Voluntary petition. A voluntary petition for bankruptcy may be filed under any chapter of the Bankruptcy Reform Act by any person who has accumulated debts which he or she is unable to pay. Certain organizations (banks, insurance companies, etc.) are prohibited from filing a voluntary petition. The petition must include the names and addresses of all secured and unsecured creditors and the amount owed each, as well as a list of all assets and property owned by the debtor.

2. Involuntary petition. The creditor of a debtor who is not paying his or her debts may force the debtor into bankruptcy by filing an involuntary petition. The petition must be signed by three or more creditors whose claims collectively

amount to at least $5,000 if the number of creditors totals twelve or more. If there are fewer than twelve creditors, the number who must sign drops to one or more whose claims total $5,000.

3. Automatic stay. Once a petition is voluntarily or involuntarily filed, the debtor is protected against any attempt made by creditors to collect a debt owed. The debtor is declared bankrupt by a court order. The bankruptcy court acquires jurisdiction over the debtor's assets.

4. Trustee's appointment and duties. The court appoints a trustee in all bankruptcy proceedings except for Chapter 7, where the trustee is selected by a vote of the creditors at their first meeting. In the latter situation, the court may appoint a receiver to be a temporary trustee until one is elected at the first meeting of the creditors.

   The trustee takes over the property of the debtor, inventories it, has it appraised, sets aside the portion exempt from execution under state or federal law as appropriate, and recovers any illegal and fraudulent transfers (such as property transferred to an unsecured creditor within ninety days preceding the date the petition was filed). Finally, he or she reduces the estate to cash to pay the creditors.

   Individuals are allowed to keep exempt assets so that they have a chance to start over. For instance, if a married couple owns their home, they may keep up to $45,000 equity in the house, plus their furniture, clothing, and other personal items up to a certain amount.

   In reorganization proceedings, the trustee must keep the debtor's business operational, and invest and distribute any income earned from the continued operation of the business.

5. First meeting of the creditors. The court will notify the creditors of the time and place of their first meeting. Before this, the creditors must each submit a claim stating the amount owed to them.

   In Chapter 7 proceedings, the creditors will elect a trustee. The debtor must attend this meeting as a requirement for having his or her debts discharged in bankruptcy. The creditors will pose questions to the debtor to discern whether the debtor has concealed or fraudulently transferred any assets.

6. Rights of creditors. After the first meeting all creditors must file proof of their claims. The legitimacy of a claim disputed

by the debtor will be evaluated by the court. A secured creditor is assured of collecting the money owed to him or her out of specific assets which had been provided by the debtor as collateral.

There is no guarantee, of course, that the proceeds from the sale of these assets will be sufficient to satisfy the debt owed. Unsecured claims follow the satisfaction of secured ones.

7. Denial of discharge. A discharge from debts may be denied under certain circumstances, such as concealing assets to defraud creditors, falsifying records, and having had a prior voluntary discharge within six years.

Chapter 13 provides for an individual to be rehabilitated without having all assets liquidated as under Chapter 7. Chapter 13 is a debt-consolidation program which allows for a full or even partial repayment of debts over a period of up to five years. It can only be filed by individuals who have total unsecured debts of less than $100,000 and total secured debts of less than $250,000.

Once a Chapter 13 plan has been approved, all creditors must stop collection efforts. They must suspend interest and late charges on most debts. Each month, the debtor turns over a specified sum of money to a court trustee, who in turn dispenses it to creditors according to the plan.

If the debtor repays at least 70% of the debts, the usual six-year period for filing again for bankruptcy is waived. Payment of claims may come out of future income only, or out of some combination of future income plus the liquidation of currently owned assets.

Considerable abuse of Chapter 7 proceedings following their revision in 1978 led to a further revamping in 1984. For instance, in determining whether a debtor's financial situation dictates a Chapter 7 filing or a Chapter 13 debt repayment, bankruptcy judges can now consider more than just a debtor's assets and liabilities. They may also consider his or her current income and expenditures.

In addition, tightening of the provisions for exemptions of

assets from liquidation has made Chapter 7 far less attractive. Thus many more debtors go the Chapter 13 route.

In Canada, a firm facing insolvency can attempt to refinance in one of two ways.

1. In receivership it can attempt to persuade its creditors, or other investors, to provide additional financing, or
2. it can make a proposal such as the *Columbian* did in the illustration above.

But the company's secured creditors can foreclose at any time.

In the U.S., firms attempting to reorganize are given some breathing room under Chapter 11 of the Bankruptcy Reform Act. The purpose of Chapter 11 is to keep the firm operating and to protect the value of its assets while a reorganization plan is worked out. The plan could be to pay creditors less than the full amount of their claims, or to pay over a larger period of time.

Companies can be granted 120 days to present the plan to creditors and another 60 days to get the plan approved. During this period other proceedings against the firm are halted. The plan is accepted if more than one-half of the creditors, holding at least two-thirds of the value of all claims, vote in favor of it.[10]

While bankruptcy proceedings have provided considerable relief to many debt-plagued individuals and companies, after-effects must be noted. In Canada, for instance, bankruptcy remains as a mark on one's credit rating for six years after the discharge. Chapter 7 filings in the U.S. remain on the credit record for ten years, Chapter 13 for seven.

Bankruptcy can also negatively affect one's ability to get a job where the employee must be bonded. Certain debts must be paid even if a discharge is secured, such as alimony, child support, and taxes. While going through the OPD program one cannot obtain further credit.

PART 3
Bankruptcy, Business Ethics, and the Bible

George Jelksma retired last April from the home-construction business he had started forty years ago with a prayer and $2,000.

At his retirement dinner, George reflected on his career. "We always worked hard to provide good quality, be honest with our customers, charge reasonable prices, and treat employees fairly," he said. "God has been good. We could provide for our children, support the church, and retire comfortably. I'm sure as my son John takes over, he'll continue our Christian standards."

A year later son John assessed his first year in charge: "I didn't know how tough this was going to be. I had taken some college courses in accounting, marketing, and personnel supervision. . . .

"But that was the easy part. You wouldn't believe the hard questions I've run into this past year. We needed better accounting records, so I planned to buy a small computer. But our bookkeeper is sixty and says he can't learn to use a personal computer at his age. I can't wait years to improve this system. So do I let him go?

"In our area, the home-construction competition is fierce.

We need better connections with large-scale housing developers. Last month a developer invited me to lunch and agreed to get us some contracts with her firm if we'd cut her in privately for 1% of our take.

"I was shocked, but she says that's how business connections are built around here now. Is there anything wrong with this? I'm under pressure. Sales and profits are down, and I've got a payroll to meet.

"We also need more advertising. My sister runs a small agency that could do the work. Should I give it to her, or is that nepotism?

"Our company doesn't carry an employee health-insurance policy. Insurance is terribly expensive, but many workers don't have personal coverage. It's legal not to cover them, but is it right?

"I also really wonder if some of our customers aren't borrowing over their heads to finance their new houses. Should I figure that's their problem and keep my nose out of it?

"I'm supposed to continue our Christian standards? I'm in over my head, and I feel all alone."

—Shirley J. Roels, "Ethics, Loneliness, and Business," *The Banner*, May 14, 1990, p. 10. Used by permission.

Chapter 5
Ethics: How? Why? Whose?

Finally Undershaft [a capitalist munitions maker], asks "Well, is there anything you know or care for?" His son replies, "I know the difference between right and wrong." "You don't say so!" exclaims Undershaft. "What, no capacity for business, no knowledge of law, no sympathy with art, no pretension to philosophy, only a simple knowledge of the secret that has puzzled all the philosophers, baffled all the lawyers, muddled all the men of business, and ruined most of the artists? The secret of right and wrong—at 24, too!"
—*Major Barbara*, George Bernard Shaw

Being a member of a public school board requires a great deal of reading, normally of a rather prosaic nature. The winter of 1985 brought a decided change to that aspect of this school trustee's life, however.

I sat at the board table with my six colleagues and our senior administrators staring in amazement at a picture of one of our female junior high teachers. She was pictured in a men's erotic magazine, dressed only in stockings, high heels, and a garter belt. Equally distressing was the fact that the photograph was identified as having been submitted by her husband, also one of our teachers.

The board conducted hearings with the teachers, suspending them for six weeks without salary on the grounds of professional misconduct. The teachers appealed to a

three-person Board of Reference under the British Columbia School Act. The majority of that board ordered them re-
instated. It labeled their activities an appalling lack of judgment but not, strictly speaking, misconduct. The School
Board took the case to the Supreme Court of British Columbia. The decision was reversed in the School Board's favor,
and subsequently upheld in the B.C. Court of Appeal.

The episode aroused considerable controversy in the
community—indeed around the province. The *Vancouver
Sun* was particularly critical of the School Board's decision to
suspend.

> When it comes to inappropriate behaviour, that kind of hypo-
> critical prudery is more suited to Harper Valley in the 1950's
> than the Fraser Valley in the 1980's. . . . Lawful private activities
> of teachers that are unrelated to teaching are none of a school
> board's business.[1]

As it happens, our school district encompasses what passes for the Bible Belt in British Columbia. Consequently,
many local politicians have strong Judeo-Christian values.
The decision to suspend, then, was unanimous despite the
public debate.

But as controversial as that particular issue was, it represents only one of the many value judgments, many with significant ethical overtones, which board members must
regularly make as they collect and spend tax dollars, and
provide for the needs of students and employees. Business
life is no different. Ethics and values play a key role in
decision-making. Williams and Houck, authors of a fine
casebook in Christian business ethics entitled *Full Value*,
note seven key value-laden business decision areas where a
biblical worldview could have a decided impact.

1. how we use power over individuals;
2. how we understand our use of nature and natural resources;

3. how we understand wealth and property;
4. how we hope to achieve happiness;
5. how we understand justice;
6. how we respond to our drive to gratify material wants;
7. how we understand time.[2]

It would not occur to many, however, that business people would care about the ethics, biblical or otherwise, of business decision-making. In fact, the term *business ethics* has often been consigned to the same category as "jumbo shrimp," "cruel kindness," or even "army intelligence." It is seen as blatant contradiction in terms.

This pessimistic view of the morality of the typical business person is illustrated again and again in public opinion and other polls. For instance, a majority of Chicago-area business executives surveyed in 1987 agreed that good ethics are good business. But more than 20% said that they would be willing to bribe a public inspector. About 73% considered practices in their own industry to be unethical.[3]

Eighty-seven percent of the managers surveyed by the National Association of Accountants indicated that they would be willing to commit fraud in certain cases. Thirty-eight percent admitted they would pad a government contract if given the opportunity.[4]

A 1983 Gallup Poll done for the *Wall Street Journal* reported that 49% of the public thought business ethical standards had declined in the past decade. Only 9% thought they had risen. Greed and selfish attitudes were cited by the general public as the most likely causes of the decline, although business executives themselves most commonly blamed the declining influence of religious and moral values.[5]

There has been a seeming explosion of ethical debates of the Ivan Boesky insider-trading sort in the 1980s. Thus it is not surprising that there has developed a parallel growth in interest in business ethics. For instance, in 1988 only 11% of American M.B.A. programs did not have an ethics course in the curriculum.[6]

Is this new emphasis likely to turn the tide? Consider the results of a survey conducted by two Columbia University business professors which attempted to evaluate the effectiveness of business ethics courses.

> Slightly more than a thousand alumni who graduated from 1953 through 1987 responded. Forty percent said they had been rewarded by their companies for doing things they found "ethically troubling." Only 20% said the reverse—that they had been rewarded for refusing to do such things.
>
> Of those who refused to do what was "ethically troubling" to them, 31% said they had been punished. Punishment ranged from a penalty to the subtle message that they were no longer important to the company.[7]

Consequently, the commercial media are prone to display a most unflattering picture of corporate life. In 200 episodes of 50 top network series, according to a Media Institute study, business people typically were portrayed in a negative manner. They were pictured as criminals, fools, or greedy or malevolent egotists 67% of the time.[8]

Many business people and writers of business texts reject this low view of the state of business ethics. One author, for instance, entitled his book *Beyond the Bottom Line: How Business Leaders Are Turning Principles into Profits.*[9] In it he cites many examples of the high ethical practices of such well-known companies as Levi Strauss, IBM, Johnson and Johnson, and Dayton Hudson.

You may be wondering if this is really necessary, a book on business ethics written for a Christian audience. Oh yes, we will all agree with the Vancouver theology professor who, in observing the modern ethical scene, remarked,

> Recent scandals seem to be making people realize it's no longer clear that we know, or can agree on what we expect of each other. . . . No one knows what's cricket anymore.[10]

But surely such quotes are applicable only to "the world," not to those who practice business while professing Christian beliefs.

Can we be so sure? Consider the following Christian business leaders who have all done well in economic life.

1. The chairman of the board of one of America's largest dry goods corporations, known for having read the Bible through at least 70 times, was interviewed by a biographical story writer for a major evangelical publication. He exclaimed, "I never mix the Bible with business. Good business is good business. There's no Christian way of doing business."[11]

2. A midwestern real estate investor talked about the profits he had made on a recent deal. While his elderly mother seemed content with getting an 8 1/2% return on their money, he laughed. "I don't go into any deals unless I can make 500-2000% profit!" he boasted.

    He went on to explain how easily this can be done. Simply find people who don't know the value of their property or are anxious to get rid of it for financial reasons. Never tell the seller the potentials for the property—or the deal you are planning. He then boasted that the Lord had been good to him in several recent deals.[12]

3. A businessman in DePere, Wisconsin, was founder and president of an investment firm. He had frequently been featured in various Wisconsin newspapers and periodicals for his uniquely Christian approach to business. He and his associates began each day with prayer and devotions, which the president cited as the foundation for his success. At the same time these people were defrauding 800 investors of 13.5 million dollars, the largest securities fraud case in Wisconsin history.[13]

4. The following are excerpts from an interview done by *Faith Today* magazine with millionaire Canadian businessman Jim Pattison while he served as chairman of Expo '86, the highly successful world's fair held in Vancouver, B.C.

    Q. What role does your Christian faith play in your work?
    A. Faith has always had a major impact on my life. But as far as the fair is concerned, we've run it as we would our business.

    Q. Is it your kind of Christian witness—your corporation?

A. Not at all. I run my business on a very business-like basis . . . on what I consider to be sound business principles, as would be normal. My business is my business. I never let politics or religion affect my business knowingly.[14]

5. This final anecdote is slightly different from the above examples, while illustrating the same point. A Christian in the development business, whom I know well, had built a number of attractive condominiums. He marketed them to the large retirement sector of my own community. The advertised price at the time was $70,000.

A recently widowed elderly lady approached the developer and offered him the advertised price. My friend sensed her inexperience at this sort of thing. He asked if she had ever made such a purchase before.

"No," she replied. "My husband always looked after our finances."

"If you had ever purchased a home" he said, "you would realize that $70,000 is just a starting figure. We would expect to sell the condominium for around $65,000."

Needless to say, the widow was happy to reduce her offer and buy the home.

When word of this incident got out, other developers in the city, many of them Christians (in fact, mostly Mennonite), ridiculed my friend for not taking the full $70,000. They called him a fool.

Apparently the need for a distinctively biblical approach to business decision-making and practice is not necessarily obvious (or desirable) to all Christian businesspeople. Does such an approach exist?

The place to begin is by asking, what does the term *ethics* mean? Apparently this is not obvious. Manuel Velasquez cites a classic study of the ethics of business managers done by Raymond Baumhart. 50% of businesspeople defined ethical as "what my feelings tell me is right." 25% defined it in religious terms as what is "in accord with my religious beliefs." 18% defined ethical as what "conforms to the golden rule."

One typical reply to Baumhart's interview went like this:

Ethical means accepted standards in terms of your personal and social welfare; what you believe is right. But what confuses me . . . is the possibility that I have been misguided, or that somebody else has been poorly educated. Maybe each of us thinks he knows what is ethical, but we differ. How can you tell who is right then?[15]

The term "ethics" is defined in various ways. One book on the subject suggests that:

> Ethics is, first of all, the quest for, and the understanding of, the good life, living well, a life worth living. It is largely a matter of perspective: putting every activity and goal in its place, knowing what is worth doing and what is not worth doing, knowing what is worth wanting and having and knowing what's not worth wanting and having.[16]

This understanding of the term appears to be shared by the *Journal of Business Ethics*. It states that "ethics is circumscribed as all human action aimed at securing a good life."[17]

Other definitions have a more explicit moral quality. One widely used textbook in the study of business and society says that:

> Ethics is a set of rules that define right and wrong conduct. These ethical rules tell us when our behavior is acceptable and when it is disapproved and considered to be wrong. Ethics deals with fundamental human relationships. Ethical rules are guides to moral behavior.[18]

Christian philosopher Arthur Holmes employs a similar approach.

> Ethics is about the good (that is, what values and virtues we should cultivate) and about the right (that is, what our moral duties may be). It examines alternative views of what is good and right; it explores ways of gaining the moral knowledge we need; it asks why we ought to do right; and it brings all this to bear on the practical moral problems that arouse such thinking in the first place.[19]

Holmes' definition will be taken as an adequate representation of the various ones consulted. All definitions put forward indicate, either explicitly or implicitly, that ethics is concerned with making moral judgments, including moral decisions as to what constitutes "the good life."[20]

How often do ethical challenges present themselves in the course of everyday business life? The average business person does not regularly deal with questions of bribery, falsification of documents, sexism, or collusion. Most businesses survive from year to year without charges of immorality. Are ethics, then, an everyday concern?

I believe they are. Go back to the seven business decision areas I earlier quoted from *Full Value*. There it is implied that ethics are (or should be) a part of regular business decision-making. Ethics should inform businesspersons' relationships with employees and other individuals, their use of natural resources, and their attitude toward the gratification of material wants which consumers may express.

There is hardly an area of business life where value judgments and trade-offs involving conflicting demands are not regularly made. This is true whether dealing with outside "constituencies" such as government, suppliers, consumers, labor markets, and society at large—or inside "constituencies" such as employees, directors, and shareholders,

Consider this scenario. A plant manager holds strongly to all of the following values:

a. Pollution is wrong and should be avoided.
b. Consumers deserve high quality at fair prices.
c. Employees should be well treated and fairly compensated.
d. Shareholders deserve an adequate return on their investment.

Suppose these values come into conflict. For instance, tighter pollution control standards may require a huge additional cost to improve pollution control at the manager's factory. The manager could lobby the regulatory agency to loosen the standards, except that she agrees with them.

But where does she come up with the money to pay for the expensive equipment needed to comply? Does she increase her products' prices? Or lessen the quality? Does she reduce the wage increase she honestly believes her employees deserve? Does she reduce the company's profit to make the owners shoulder the whole cost?

This simplified scenario pales in comparison to such complicated decision-making processes as were present when the deadly gas leak at Union Carbide's plant in India killed 2,000 people, or when the Exxon Valdez oil spill caused incredible pollution off Alaska's coast. But it illustrates that even in less dramatic situations, value judgments must be made. Questions of right and wrong, good and bad, must be addressed. Compromises among values, all dearly held, must occur. The question is, how should ethical decisions be made?

Ask the person on the street how she or he thinks business decisions are made and the response will likely be, "Only if there's also a buck in it for the businessperson!" Such a conclusion is certainly tempting. Consider the reasons given for ethical decision-making in a recent issue of the *Canadian Business Review*.

> Ethics are definitely important to business for several reasons. Ethical behaviour is now a necessity if you want to do business with some governments, banks and other corporations that require compliance disclosures from suppliers. . . . In addition, opportunities to profit from ethical corporate behaviour are becoming evident. Examples include Loblaw's (a supermarket chain) green products and Dofasco (a large steel company) finding that recycling waste water actually produces a reasonable payback.

The article does admit that such self-interested reasons for being ethical do fall short of idealism.

However, these are relatively crass reasons for declaring business ethics to be important. There are also altruistic benefits from good ethical performance that should not be minimized, as well as benefits to society in general.[21]

It is difficult, however, to arrive at any other conclusion than that self-interest guides business ethical decision-making.

Just recently I received literature from an organization of ethical consultants whose purpose it is to assist corporations with the management of their activities. I will leave the firm unnamed, but what follows is a representative sample of reasons for subscribing to their service.

> Today's legislators are zeroing in on you. They're trying to hold you *personally liable for the actions of your corporation*. And not just fiduciary matters. They're adding the environment, hiring practices, product liability, and other social concerns to the list.
>
> Your responsibilities are being steadily expanded to embrace individual shareholders, employees, government, creditors, and even the community at large.
>
> Make no mistake about it. *All eyes are focused on you.*
>
> This pioneering newsletter gives you the information you need *to keep legal trapdoors from snapping shut on you.* [Emphasis is that of the company.]

I have no quarrel with their purpose or the service they are selling. I am only illustrating the point that the motivation is not that ethics are right in some fundamental way, but that a firm will be punished or lose a competitive edge for not following them. But is self-interest the only ethical approach that businesspeople use?

Types of Ethical Reasoning

There seem to be as many frameworks for ethical analysis as there are writers on the subject. I have no desire to add to the list. What follows is a summary of the primary ways in which businesspeople appear to think about ethical decisions.

Utilitarian ethics: what benefits the most people is right

The first major ethical decision-making orientation of businesspeople is tied up with the consequences of one's actions. It is usually referred to as *utilitarianism*. Those who affirm utilitarianism want to maximize benefits (or utility) for the greatest number of people.

> If the benefits that result from a decision outweigh the costs, then the action is said to be "good." If a businessperson is considering a number of options, the option with the highest net benefit would be the "right" one to pursue. To pursue any other course of action, even if it, too, had a positive net benefit, would be "wrong."[22]

Utilitarianism, then, is goal- or consequence-based. In approaching ethical questions it asks, "What action or policy maximizes the benefit/cost relationship?" In so doing, it seeks the greatest good (or lowest cost where only costs result) for the greatest number of people.

Moral rules about honoring contracts, promise-keeping, collusion, and so on are promoted as maximizing benefits (or utility) in the long run, rather than being inherently right. To accomplish this, one must somehow reduce to measurable units the quantity of benefits (both direct and indirect) produced by one's actions and subtract the units of harm the action produces.

In making these calculations, one considers the impact of an action on all affected parties. One then chooses the action whose overall benefits are greatest in comparison to any alternative action. Ideally, one is to refrain from any self-interest in making one's calculations.

With respect to moral rules, then, a utilitarian would normally reject lying because of the negative effects lying tends to have on human welfare. But if a lie could be shown to be a more beneficial choice in a certain situation, one would resort to lying on that occasion.

Thus, utilitarian philosopher J. J. C. Smart reasons that

> Moral rules, on the extreme utilitarian view, are rules of thumb only. . . . If we do come to the conclusion that we should break the rule and if we have weighed in the balance our own fallibility and liability to personal bias, what good reason remains for keeping the rule?[23]

The final appeal with respect to ethical decision-making is this: do the consequences of a decision show, through appropriate measurements, the promotion of the greatest good as compared to any other possible decision? As to what constitutes "the good," utilitarians differ. One of the theory's originators, Jeremy Bentham (1748-1832), saw the good as pleasure (versus pain). John Stuart Mill argued for the dignity and desirability of what is distinctive about humans. A more recent philosopher, G. E. Moore, understood the good as an intuitive concept which includes a great variety of cultural and social satisfactions one would desire for their own sake.

Such an approach has obvious appeal to businesspeople involved in a market system, since the market is, for a host of typical business decisions, the ultimate determiner of the cost/benefit relationship. Questions concerning production and distribution of goods and services, pricing, effective advertising and promotion techniques, wages, and financing are all answered by the impersonal forces of the marketplace. There is little concern with absolute standards other than the absolute of maximizing net benefit for the most people (including oneself, usually!). One ethics text sees this liberation from absolutes as a decided improvement.

Ethics isn't a set of absolute principles, divorced from and imposed on everyday life. Ethics is a way of life, a seemingly delicate but in fact very strong tissue of endless adjustments and compromises. It is the awareness that one is an intrinsic part of a social order, in which the interests of others and one's own interests are inevitably intertwined. And what is business . . . if not precisely that awareness of what other people want and need, and how you yourself can prosper by providing it? Businesses great and small prosper because they respond to people, and fail when they do not respond . . . Ethics is the art of mutually agreeable tentative compromise. Insisting on absolute principles is, if I may be ironic, unethical.[24]

As repugnant as the above perspective may seem to many Christians, utilitarianism is an important avenue for ethical analysis in North American business. For instance, Christian businessman Jim Pattison (mentioned earlier) can say that

I never let . . . religion affect my business knowingly. If I did, I wouldn't distribute Communist books (one of his companies distributes books and magazines) . . . I don't agree with Communist ideas, but if people in a free society want to write about Communists, *then we distribute if the public wants them.* So you let the market decide. [Emphasis is mine.][25]

It should be mentioned that Pattison's company was also a major distributor of pornographic magazines, including the one in which appeared the picture of the nude teacher (discussed above).

This same desire to avoid thorny questions concerning absolute right and wrong appears in an article about swimsuit magazines. Most of us are aware of the famous (or infamous) *Sports Illustrated* swimsuit issue. *SI* normally sells 3 million copies of any one issue, with revenues amounting to something under $7 million. The swimwear issue realizes nearly double the circulation and more than triple the revenue.

A competitor and imitator of its bathing suit publication,

Inside Sports, achieves similar sales improvements with its version. The publisher, when questioned about the ethical issue of sexploitation, replied, "I don't think in terms of sexism. I think in terms of what our readers want."[26]

Even as esteemed (in some circles) a theologian as Harold Lindsell lends inadvertent support to this notion that the amoral market should be the final arbiter of good and bad business behavior. While castigating socialist enemies of the market system who would impose absolute notions of what people need, he makes the following remarkable (naive?) statement.

> Free enterprise recognizes man's self-interest (a quality which, when balanced by altruism is not illegitimate) and uses it for the good of the many. He who becomes wealthy *by making available to people what they want* can hardly be an enemy of society [emphasis added].[27]

The tobacco companies should emblazon this sentiment on their cigarette packages to counterbalance the Surgeon General's warnings!

Not everyone is comfortable with an ethical system based solely on whether the consequences of decisions can be shown to maximize benefits for a majority.

> Locked as we are into a market economy, the tendency to see every issue in terms of costs becomes overwhelming. But one shies away from the idea that moral behavior is a function of dollars and cents.[28]

> Businesspeople are used to thinking about benefit/cost analysis in terms of the net benefit to the client or their own firm—ethical analysis must go beyond that.[29]

Objections to utilitarian ethics

Objections to utilitarianism typically run along two lines. The first has to do with the measurement of utility (or benefit, or happiness). Just how does one calculate utility? And for whom does one measure it? Can self-interest be avoided in deciding which is the appropriate group who is to benefit? Business decision-makers are ultimately accountable for how their *own* firms benefit. How are they then to make an objective appraisal of *societal* benefit from actions they are contemplating?

The second objection concerns the minority who lose out in the calculation. Do they have rights? Does the majority become a tyrant, with issues of fairness lost in the shuffle?

Velasquez beautifully sets out the difficulties in actually making calculations of benefits and costs. He raises four objections.

1. How can the utilities that different actions have for different people be measured and compared as utilitarianism requires? Suppose you and I would both enjoy getting a certain job. How can we figure out whether the utility you would get out of having the job is more or less than the utility I would get out of having it? Each of us may be sure that he or she would benefit most from the job, but since we cannot get into each other's skin, this judgment has no objective basis.
2. Some benefits and costs seem virtually impossible to measure. How, for example, can one measure the value of health and life in deciding on pollution issues?
3. Because many of the benefits and costs of an action cannot be reliably predicted, they also cannot be adequately measured. What are the likely benefits of investments in the space program, or medical research?
4. It is unclear exactly what to count as a "benefit" and as a "cost." How would different cultural groups view a bank loan to the owners of an x-rated theater, for instance, or a gay bar—as a benefit to society or a cost?[30]

Beyond these considerations, Arthur Holmes asks just which consequences should be considered. Only the intended consequences? Other predictable consequences as well? Or just the actual consequences (which can be measured, of course, only after the fact)?

Does the average person have sufficient access to the needed information (if it exists at all) to make the calculations? Is it enough to take the sum of all the surplus of good over bad for all the people involved? Should one calculate an average across an entire population? Or should different segments be considered separately?[31]

The measurement difficulties could be elaborated on. But for the Christian, perhaps the greater objection is that utilitarianism does not finally recognize individual rights, nor does it deal adequately with distributive justice.

I have often heard arguments between those who oppose pornography and those who either profit by or at least tolerate it. The arguments center on the allegation that pornography is wrong because it harms society in some way (say, through increasing the incidence of rape and child sexual abuse). This is a utilitarian approach. It argues a moral case on the basis of calculations of the virtually incalculable. It could instead argue along some other line, such as that pornography is an attack on the inherent dignity of a person created in God's image. It turns the full-orbed individual into a one-dimensional sex object. A utilitarian approach, by itself, overlooks the notion that something is inherently right or wrong regardless of consequences.

Consequences are important to the Christian of course, as we know from such passages as John 15 (JB).

> Every branch in me that bears no fruit he cuts away (v. 2).
> Whoever remains in me, with me in him, bears fruit in plenty (v. 5).
> It is to the glory of my Father that you should bear much fruit, and then you will be my disciples (v. 8).
> I commissioned you to go out and to bear fruit, fruit that will last (v. 16).

Certainly one indication of the excellence of our spiritual lives is the consequences of our actions. In fact, Paul tells us that we are created in Christ Jesus to do good works (Eph. 2:10). And James warns that any claim to a living faith without outward evidence is false (James 2:14-17).

But at other times we see spiritual giants plugging away at doing God's will even when no good consequence can be detected. Jeremiah, who early in his ministry referred to God as "the spring of living water" (Jer. 2:13), laments that his efforts have come to nothing and his lot seems undeserved.

> Think of how I suffer reproach for your sake . . .
> O Lord God Almighty.
>
> I never sat in the company of revelers, never made merry with them; I sat alone because your hand was on me and you had filled me with indignation.
>
> Why is my pain unending and my wound grievous and incurable?
>
> Will you be to me like a deceptive brook, like a spring that fails? (15:15-18).

Jeremiah, as we know, died in obscurity, with little to show for his 40 years of prophesying, although his commitment to God's calling seldom wavered. He put up with every sort of indignity and threat, including rejection by his own family and neighbors (11:21; 12:6). Certainly it was not the favorable consequences of his actions that kept him going (although great benefit for the Jewish nation is what he sought). He was instead driven by belief in the inherent rightness of his cause, a conviction grounded in God's word to him.

Deontological ethics: some things are inherently right

Other frameworks for ethical analysis focus on this notion that something is inherently right or just, regardless of the consequences. Such approaches are *deontological*. This comes from the Greek word for "obligation." Rather than beneficial results determining moral duty, certain acts are, in themselves, worthy of respect. This is true whether or not adhering to them would maximize the good for the greatest number.

One such approach emphasizes the rights of individuals. According to utilitarian thinking, if an action benefits the greatest number it is ethical—even if this action deprives a minority of those benefits or of any right to an alternative course of action. An approach based on individual rights accords respect to each and every individual who may be influenced by an action.

The concept of a right can be defined in various ways. For instance, it can refer to a person being *authorized* or *empowered* to do something on his or her own behalf or on behalf of others. For example, private property rights allow the owner to do what he or she wishes with the property.

Or the term can be used to indicate that other people may not restrict individuals from pursuing their own self-interests. This use of the term could be illustrated by constitutional guarantees of freedom of association.

A closed union shop might be seen, for instance, as a violation of one's fundamental right to associate (or *not* associate). A group of workers who band together in a closed shop with compulsory membership may receive material benefits from this. But such benefits do not justify denying the individual's right to free association. Thus the United Nations' *Universal Declaration of Human Rights* declares that "no one may be compelled to belong to an association."[32]

Eighteenth-century philosopher Immanuel Kant has provided one of the best-known bases for establishing moral rights. Called the Categorical Imperative, it puts forward the following principles, as summarized by Velasquez.

1. An action is morally right for a person in a certain situation if and only if the person's reason for carrying out the action is a reason that he or she would be willing to have every person act on, in any similar situation.

This principle accords *equal* rights and respect to each individual. It argues that what is morally right for me to do must be equally morally right for any other person.

2. An action is morally right for a person if and only if, in performing the action, the person does not use others merely as a means for advancing his or her own interests, but also both respects and develops their capacity to choose freely for themselves.

This principle respects the inherent dignity of each and every individual, demanding that people never be exploited for one's own self-interests.[33]

As attractive as these principles are to Christians who believe in the golden rule and the inherent value of individuals as God's image-bearers, they still leave us with a question. What particular moral rights do human beings have?

Holmes suggests that "the clue is to know what is essential to being a human person." He sees justification for philosopher John Locke's three natural rights: life, liberty, and property.

1. The right to life obviously is prerequisite to all else.
2. The right to liberty respects the self-determination of one endowed with the capacity for deliberation and free choice.
3. The right to property is concerned that the fruits of one's labor should meet basic needs and sustain a human quality of life.

To these Holmes adds the right to whatever is necessary "for life and godliness," such as freedom of information, freedom of association, freedom of religion, and so on. He notes that in every case one's particular rights must be limited by the equal rights of others.[34]

Depending on one's religious or philosophical presuppositions, conclusions concerning what constitutes inherent moral rights may differ. But most North Americans share a common view of a broad range of individual moral rights.

Problems with "rights-based" ethics

We are left with three difficulties. First, how does one choose among conflicting individual rights? This concern comes up repeatedly in the pro-life versus pro-choice debate. One side puts the right to life of a fetus over the right to privacy. Another puts control of the mother's body first.

Second, human rights consider the individual at the expense of societal well-being. Utilitarianism, of course, does the opposite. But there are times when the interests of society as a whole may require denying individual rights. An example is the denial of civil rights during times of war or other emergencies. When does the need for majority benefit overwhelm an individual's rights? Arguments over the appropriate amount of intrusion into the private sector by the government turn on this point.

Third, rights, as well as utilitarianism, ignore questions of the just or fair distribution of society's benefits and burdens among all people.

> Justice (or fairness) exists when benefits and burdens are distributed equitably and according to some accepted rule. For society as a whole, social justice means that a society's income and wealth are distributed among the people in fair proportions. A fair distribution does not necessarily mean an equal distribution. The shares received by the population depend on the society's approved rules for getting and keeping income and wealth. These rules will vary from society to society. Most societies try to consider people's needs, abilities, efforts, and the contributions they make to society's welfare. Since these factors are seldom equal, fair shares will vary from person to person and from group to group.[35]

The above definition refers to that category of justice called *distributive* justice. This refers to the fair distribution of society's benefits and burdens. Current controversial examples include the issue of equal pay for work of equal value, and the difference in wage rates between men and women.

Other categories include *retributive* justice, the just imposition of penalties on wrongdoers; and *compensatory* justice, the fair compensation for wrongful loss of something to another.

In capitalistic economies the prevailing view is that society's benefits should be distributed primarily on the basis of a person's contribution to society's well-being, measured in terms of such things as effort and productivity. Socialists are more inclined to see benefits going in the direction of need.

Justice: the Bible's contribution to ethical reasoning

Justice is an important Old Testament theme, often linked with the word "righteousness." Justice is rightness rooted in God's character, and ought to be an attribute of human beings. Wise persons speak it (Ps. 37:30) and think it (Prov. 12:5). God requires it of humankind (Mic. 6:8). The righteous enjoy it (Prov. 21:15).[36]

We modern North Americans tend to think in terms of *getting* justice in a *court of law*. But in Old Testament times one *did* justice in a variety of arenas, including economic, social, family, and religious contexts.

Jeremiah offers insight into what it means to be a follower of God and seek justice. Beginning in chapter 22 of his prophesy, we read a series of assessments of various Judean kings, each a son or grandson of the great and godly Josiah. All feel the lash of Jeremiah's tongue, none more than Jehoiakim, the king who sought Jeremiah's life.

> Woe to him who builds his palace by unrighteousness,
> his upper rooms by injustice,
> making his countrymen work for nothing,
> not paying them for their labor.
> He says, "I will build myself a great palace
> with spacious upper rooms."
> So he makes large windows in it,
> panels it with cedar
> and decorates it in red.
> Does it make you a king
> to have more and more cedar?
> Did not your father have food and drink?
> *He did what was right and just,*
> so all went well with him.
> He defended the cause of the poor and needy,
> and so all went well.
> *"Is that not what it means to know me?*
> *declares the LORD.*
> But your eyes and your heart
> are set only on dishonest gain,
> on shedding innocent blood
> and on oppression and extortion (22:13-17).

At the time this prophecy was uttered, Judah was a vassal kingdom of Egypt. Thus the impoverished Judeans paid taxes to both their own and the Egyptian rulers. Josiah, Jehoiakim's father, *did justice,* defined as *defending the cause of people on the margins of society.* Jehoiakim, on the other hand, further exploited the poor, building himself a palace at their expense.

Justice, used in this way, goes beyond dispassionate fairness. It is fairness plus mercy. Justice is love in action.[37] A similar understanding is taught in James 1:27. "Religion that God our Father accepts as pure and faultless is this: *to look after orphans and widows in their distress* and to keep oneself from being polluted by the world [emphasis added]."

An even more graphic example of this Old Testament depiction of justice at work in the kingdom of God is provided by Jesus in response to John the Baptist's query. "Are you the one who was to come, or should we expect someone else?" (Luke 7:19). Our Lord replied,

> Go back and report to John what you have seen and heard: The blind receive sight, the lame walk, those who have leprosy are cured, the deaf hear, the dead are raised, and the good news is preached to the poor (Luke 7:22-23).

Arthur Holmes has seized on the Old Testament notion of justice as the key to developing a Christian ethic. He notes,

> We need an independent principle of justice to ensure an equitable distribution of good, in addition to the principle of love or benevolence that maximizes good consequences.[38]

Holmes goes on to note that justice and love do not conflict but rather supplement and reinforce one another.

> As love is obligated in justice to distribute its benefits equitably, rather than playing favorites or practicing discrimination and unfairness, so justice is motivated by love to keep its relentless quest tirelessly alive.[39]

How does justice differ from utilitarian reasoning? Both take a broad societal view. Both face the challenge of measuring costs and benefits.

Consider this true scenario. A famous businessman who got his start as an automobile dealer used to add up the sales volume of each of his salespersons. Then he fired the salesman producing the lowest volume for that month, unless the volume was particularly good.[40]

Utilitarian thinking tries to calculate the effect of a decision on all affected parties and choose the action with the greatest net benefit. Thus firing the salesmen could be seen as ethical—provided that the net benefit to customers, shareholders, other salespersons, and so on was the greatest. Standards of justice might lead one to question whether the low man on the totem pole was bearing a fair share of making the dealership a success. The first approach is interested in the *net sum*. The latter cares about *just or fair shares*.

Outlined thus far are two basic frameworks for ethical analysis. The first, called *teleological* from the Greek word for *aim* or *goal*, includes utilitarianism. It has to do with the beneficial or harmful consequences of behavior.

The second, referred to as *deontological* from the Greek word for *obligation* or *duty*, includes approaches based on fundamental human rights and standards of justice. These emphasize the inherent rightness of actions, or duty, without taking consequences into consideration.

A mixed ethical framework

None of these approaches seems sufficient, by itself, to guide the businessperson through the difficult ethical decisions he or she faces in the marketplace. There could be times when societal benefits are the preeminent concern. On other occasions questions of rights and justice may dominate.

To deal with this difficulty, some ethicists have proposed a mixed framework for ethical analysis which blends the respective positions.

Within both the Judeo-Christian heritage and that of Islam the *divine command* theory is dominant.

> For this framework, the criterion or test of right and wrong is the will of God, expressed either through nature or through revelation. It is a mixed framework because the duties or commandments associated with it are almost universally held to include elements of both teleological and deontological thinking. Often this mixture is expressed by pointing to such attributes of God's nature as benevolence, justice and mercy. . . . The divine command theory implies that actions and norms get their legitimacy from being in accord with God's will and from no other source.[41]

Holmes' approach (which was discussed earlier), involving the wedding of justice and benevolence, is a good example of such a mixed framework.

We have surveyed three avenues for ethical analysis. Are we now left with interesting theories, safely stored in an ivory tower? Is any one framework adequate to meet the needs of everyday business decision-making? Or is a mixed framework, such as the divine command theory traditionally employed by Christians, the best response to ethical challenges? Answers to these questions are the objective of the next chapter.

Chapter 6
Out of the Ivory Tower and into the Marketplace

A successful missionary has to make his theology walk in the gutter.
> —Kurt Ruby, former missionary to Colombia, South America

As both a university professor and a lay preacher, I occupy two fields often criticized for being walled off from the "real world" (whatever that is). Ethicists often face the same charge. This chapter will try to scale that wall around the ivory tower and bring ethical theory to bear on the real world of economic life.

The conclusion in Chapter 5 was that various frameworks for ethical analysis have been devised—but none is sufficient, by itself, to tackle everyday business problems.

Combining Consequences, Rights, and Justice

Most business ethicists agree that some kind of contingent approach is necessary.[1] In other words, a method must be found whereby all three major ways of doing ethical thinking—consequences, rights, and justice—can be applied either singly or in some appropriate combination.

A magnificent attempt at making ethics practical appears in an article by Professor Laura Nash, then of Harvard University's Graduate School of Business. She provides a number of questions which could be asked in any situation involving business ethics. Nash feels that the answers would help decision-makers come to sound ethical conclusions. A sampling of her questions indicates her concern for consequences, rights, and justice.

1. *Have you defined the problem accurately?* One must be careful to define fully the factual implications of a decision without letting one's loyalties sway one's objectivity.
2. *How would you define the problem if you stood on the other side of the fence?* This question provides a further check on defining a problem in a solely self-interested fashion.
3. *How did this situation occur in the first place?* Here Nash is advising decision-makers to distinguish between symptoms (a manager being ruthless with employees, or fudging the books) and the actual disease (such as intense profit pressures imposed on the manager).
4. *To whom and to what do you give your loyalty as a person and as a member of the corporation?* Nash admits that there are few automatic answers to this question, although she notes that many young managers are giving more weight to individual rather than to corporate identity.
5. *What is your intention in making this decision?*
6. *How does this intention compare with the probable results?* The reason for a company's actions will have wide-ranging effects both inside and outside the corporation. It could affect such things as attitudes toward employees and the community, wages paid, and so on. In addition, high-flown intentions may falter quickly if the project is unrealistic.
7. *Whom could your decision or action injure?* Answers to this question could lead to a decision not to act, for instance.
8. *Can you discuss the problem with the affected parties before you make your decision?* Such an approach could provide important information in answering question 7 above.
9. *Are you confident that your position will be as valid over a long period of time as it seems now?* Time alters circumstances, and few corporations are immune to shifts in financial status, external political pressure, and personnel. Nash advises that one must ask, are hard times the ultimate test of a statement of objectives, or are they a clear indication that a corporation has to be able to "afford" ethical positions?

10. *Could you disclose without qualm your decision or action to your boss, your CEO, the board of directors, your family, or society as a whole?* Disclosure is a way of sounding out one's conscience and searching out loyalties.

Nash goes on to address the question of what conditions would allow for exceptions to one's normal ethical stand. She concludes with a discussion of the proper moral standpoint of a corporation.[2]

A shorter, but also thought-provoking scheme, is suggested by Walter Kiechel in *Fortune* magazine. Starting with the utilitarian perspective, Kiechel tells the decision-maker to list the different people or groups which will be affected by the decision under consideration. He then challenges the businessperson to assess how possible different choices will affect others.

Like Nash, Kiechel advises us to ask the potentially affected parties what *they* think of the alternatives. Kiechel does not say so, but presumably these groups will respond in a self-interested fashion (most do!). This still leaves the decision-maker responsible to decide which responses have the greater merit.

Assigning priorities to the parties is the next step. One would make a decision after asking two questions: (1) How much will each party be affected? (2) What duty is owed to each party, depending on whether customers, shareholders, employees, or society at large are in view?

Based upon this series of rather subjective assessments, decision-makers now decide what action to take.

Recognizing that utilitarian considerations on their own are insufficient, the author suggests that the competing choices be measured against some standard of justice. He cites two general standards of justice: (1) Act to maximize the benefit to the least advantaged in society, or at least to do them no harm. (2) Act so that other people's ability to lead their lives as they wish is enhanced, not limited.[3]

One final example will illustrate both the value and the complication of using the contingent approach. Frederick and his colleagues suggest that if one wants to know whether a decision is ethical or unethical, one should answer three questions: (1) Do benefits exceed costs? (2) Are human rights respected? (3) Are benefits and costs fairly distributed?

If the answers are unanimously "yes," the decision is probably ethical. If the unanimous answer is "no," the decision is probably unethical. The authors are realistic, however, in assessing their own recommended method.

> What happens if the Unanimity Rule does not apply? What if there are two "yes's" and one "no," or another combination of the various possibilities? In that case, a choice is necessary. The analyst . . . then has to assign priorities to the three methods of ethical reasoning. What is most important to the analyst . . . utility? rights? or justice? What ranking should they be given? A judgment must be made, and priorities must be determined. *Unfortunately, there are no easy ways to do this* [emphasis is mine] . . . There is a natural tendency for managers . . . to assign a high priority to those things that benefit their company and preserve their jobs.[4]

Finding Guidance Beyond Self-interest

The great amount of subjectivity in all the systems we have examined leaves decision-makers with no final assurance that they are making good ethical decisions. Where so many gray areas exist, businesspeople are thrown back on their own convictions. How does one deal with the temptation to make a wholly self-interested final decision (assuming, of course, that self-interest may at times be inappropriate)?

In this situation Christian businesspeople have a decided advantage. Their belief in a higher source of moral rules and underlying principles gives them a sound foundation for making value decisions. This advantage is frankly admitted in one business ethics text.

The great religions derive their moral precepts not only from human experience but from divine revelation. Ethics must rely on the unaided human reason. Because of this, the conclusions of ethics often fall far short of the ethical imperatives found in both Judaism and Christianity. Yet, there should be no conflict between ethics and moral theology, for ethics admits its incompleteness and sends religious people to their faith for the completion of moral equipment.[5]

Arthur Holmes ably demonstrates the significance of this assertion as he discusses the structure of ethical theory. Ethics are structured utilizing four ingredients: (1) *particular cases*, such as whether a firm should declare bankruptcy; (2) *moral rules* such as those which would apply to the payment of debts; (3) *underlying principles*, including those having to do with truthfulness, faithfulness in meeting obligations, and acting justly toward lenders and employees; and (4) *one's theological or philosophical bases or presuppositions*, which in the case of the Christian are the commands of God.[6]

Whether or not one is Christian, the factual analysis of a particular case could be done in a similar manner, using a thorough system such as the Nash approach (discussed earlier). But principles, along with the specific moral rules drawn from them, may differ, depending on one's presuppositions.

Moral principles, the most inclusive and ultimate ethical concepts, apply not just to particular kinds of activities but universally—to every kind of involvement, whatever it may be. They are therefore exceptionless principles which can never give way to something more inclusive and which must never give way to expediency. "What does the Lord require . . . but to do justice, and to love kindness, and to walk humbly with your God?" (Micah 6:8). We are never exempted from acting with justice and love.[7]

Uncovering the Bible's Business Principles

As was previously discussed, not all Christians believe

that the Bible gives business decision-makers specific guidance. Perhaps their view of Scripture limits its application to specialized areas such as church, missions, and aspects of family life—rather than the complicated affairs of the business world. Such a view seriously underestimates the scope and power of God's Word.

Yet I believe few Christians would baldly assert that the Bible is limited. I suspect the problem lies in a lack of teaching on how to extract timeless biblical principles from the various forms in which biblical material is cast.

Many of the principles of human rights and justice we hold dear are not spelled out in Scripture. Rather, they have to be induced from the many applications, case studies, analogies, and figures of speech employed by the biblical writers.

What principles was Paul trying to teach about appropriate social conduct in his discussion of meat sacrificed to idols? (1 Cor. 8, 10). What do we learn about the transformation of a woman's role in church and society from Paul's discussion of her hat? (1 Cor. 11). What did Jesus mean concerning radical discipleship when he told his apostles to hate their parents? (Luke 14:26). Where in the Bible is slavery explicitly taught as wrong? Or monogamy as right? Or democracy as worth fighting for? Or abortion as unacceptable? None are readily apparent—but we believe they are there, nonetheless.

Concerning coming to ethical conclusions about business decisions, I believe the Bible functions in at least three ways. First, it gives us a *worldview,* a life perspective. In a classic article in *Harvard Business Review,* Harold L. Johnson makes this point well.

> The application of religion's ultimate insights to specific situations is, of course, a tremendously difficult task. There are no blueprints, no simple rules to go by. Christianity does not present the executive with a tool kit of easy-to-use rules and pre-

cepts by which problems can be solved. The doctrines are not bound up in a simple list of "do's" and "don'ts" somewhat in the style of a book of etiquette, which if followed will result in harmonious, gentlemanly relations within and without a business. But it does offer a *frame of reference,* a universe view, which instead of giving peace of mind and easy success in human relations often breaches the barricade of self-assurance, focuses on difficulties, and erases naive hopes of business progress ever onward, ever upward.[8]

The Bible teaches us to view society as God does, with a bird's eye, above and outside our culture (no easy task, we all agree)—rather than with the worm's eye, inside and immersed in our culture. The North American perspective, believe it or not, is not always the same as the biblical one. Anyone who has traveled to other countries, or talked to visitors from other cultures, quickly realizes how bound up we get in our particular cultural point of view. The Bible, if we let it, forces us to break through cultural conditioning.

The difficulty, of course, is that the Bible does not offer us naked biblical principles. They are instead wrapped in the clothing of their own ancient cultures.

The task of the preacher/teacher is to understand the culture in which an Old or New Testament principle is applied, strip off that old cultural exterior, and extract the biblical principle lurking underneath. To apply the Scriptures to the modern phenomenon of bankruptcy, this is what I will have to do in succeeding chapters.

The second function of Scripture is to teach us *values* which apply to business life. Values represent our ideals concerning how things ought to be, or should be done. They are inextricably bound up with ethics.

It is possible, as we discussed earlier, that equally valid values may conflict, calling us to set priorities or compromise. Ethical theory tries to help decision-makers assign those priorities. Nevertheless, a large number of relevant values can be found in Scripture, as we shall see.

Third, the Bible provides us with *general ethical principles*—comprehensive and fundamental laws or doctrines which govern the Christian's life. We may value good government, law and order, and tolerance, but sometimes a fundamental biblical principle might force us to challenge both government and law.

> Then [the Sanhedrin] called [Peter and John] in again and commanded them not to speak or teach at all in the name of Jesus. But Peter and John replied, "Judge for yourselves whether it is right in God's sight to obey you rather than God. For we cannot help speaking about what we have seen and heard" (Acts 4:18-20).

Values and moral rules are *ranked according to their centrality to underlying biblical principles*.

Now I want to consider seven Judeo-Christian values that stand in stark contrast to typical North American free enterprise values. Then I will put forward what I think is a fundamental biblical principle having to do with the key purposes of economic activity. I hope this will offer a way to start developing a thoroughgoing biblical worldview which can help sort out business ethical problems.

In our culture, certain values have developed over time. Because they are broadly accepted, their practice is continuously reinforced—holding them will normally meet with the approval of others. As I write, France is celebrating the two hundredth anniversary of the French Revolution, with its commitment to freedom, equality, and brotherhood values Western democracies continue to cherish. Many of our society's values derive from our Judeo-Christian heritage as well.

Values are not necessarily fixed, of course, although they change slowly. In some areas of thinking and conduct, values have become increasingly relative. The reasoning of the Supreme Court justice in upholding my school board's suspension of two teachers I told of earlier is an excellent example.

> A teacher is an important member of the community who leads by example. He or she not only owes a duty of good behaviour to the School Board as the employer but also to the local community at large and to the teaching profession. An appropriate standard of moral conduct or behaviour must be maintained both inside and outside the classroom. *The nature of that standard will of course vary from case to case.* Moral standards are those of the community where the teacher is employed and lives not those of some other city or municipality. In most instances there will be little difference, but what may be acceptable in an urban setting may occasionally be misconduct in a rural community and visa versa. For example, a small religious community might find it unacceptable for a female teacher to live with a man out of wedlock. . . . On the other hand, these kinds of relationships may be tolerated in an urban setting where the two people are lost in the anonymity of the crowd, because they live far away from the school or *because the values of the city are different from the values of the country* [emphasis added].[9]

I recommend the ethics casebook *Full Value*, by Williams and Houck of Notre Dame University. They, like myself, are convinced that there is a set of *fixed* biblical values which represent a desperately needed corrective to many commonly held business values.

These values shape the way a Christian sees business issues and also provide standards to guide decision-makers.[10]

Judeo-Christian Value	Contrasting Value
1. Value of power over individuals as service to help others develop their unique gifts (Phil. 2:1-18; John 13:1-14).	Value of power over individuals as domination and control of others.

2. Value of power over nature as a stewardship by persons over God's world. Persons are called to transform nature in harmony with the whole of creation (Gen. 1:26-31).

   Value of power over nature as a mandate to produce a maximum of consumer goods and creature comforts.

3. Value of wealth and property as an opportunity for increased service for humankind, yet as a possible obstacle to salvation (Luke 16:19-31; 12:13-21; Mark 12:41-44).

   Value of wealth and property as the measure of a person's worth.

4. Value of happiness as achieved through following God's intentions for humankind (Mark 8:36).

   Value of happiness as achieved through acquiring possessions.

5. Value of justice as the right of each person to the means of leading a human life (Acts 2:42-47; Lev. 25:1-55; Gal. 3:27-28).

   Value of justice as the protection of property already possessed.

6. Value of deferring gratification of wants (John 12:23-26; Luke 14:27; Matt. 16:24; 10:39).

   Value of immediate gratification of wants.

7. Value of time as reverence for God (Luke 12:22-32).	Value of time as money.

If implemented in personal and corporate policies, these values would affect many areas of business life. Among these would be human relations, whether involving employees, unions, customers, suppliers, lenders, shareholders, or society at large; marketing strategies, including what products and services to offer and appropriate advertising content; environmental concerns; corporate strategy; social responsibility; and the general pursuit of profit.

Applying Judeo-Christian Values

Following are four examples of the adoption of Judeo-Christian values and their impact on normal business practices. Three are from the management side and the other one is from labor.

In 1978, businessman David Simmonds fell out with his partners over the issue of rewarding certain key employees. Simmonds, a Baptist, felt that senior people who had made a substantial contribution to the company's success deserved to share in the ownership of the company. His partners preferred a closely held structure.

Accordingly, Simmonds pulled out of the company and started his own firm, near Toronto, taking those key senior people with him. His company has grown from 42 to 150 employees, with sales increasing from $5.12 million in 1979 to $34.6 million in 1987. True to his original principles, 14 of the employees own shares. Simmonds attributes his success to people.

> In our approach to business, relationships are the most important to us—relationships with our suppliers, staff and customers. . . . We'll go the second mile in accommodating staff or accommodating customers in credit decisions. There are times when our hearts rule our heads.[11]

Another example of the impact of biblical values on the mission and policies on a business comes from Chicago. ServiceMaster was founded by another devout Baptist, Marion E. Wade, as a cleaning service for homes and offices in the 1950s. Today under the leadership of two outstanding evangelicals, Chairman Kenneth T. Wessner and President C. William Pollard, the company earns revenues in excess of $1 billion per year while providing extensive services to more than 1,000 American hospitals. ServiceMaster can outfit a hospital with virtually everything it needs except doctors and nurses.[12]

In an unpublished paper, Pollard notes that there are a variety of reasons why people work. For some, it is simply a necessary evil; for others, it is a means to some end, such as materialistic accomplishments, power, or social status. But some people value work as a special calling, a Christian ministry. This, he says, is ServiceMaster's view.

> ServiceMaster provides a unique opportunity for our work to be both an individual and corporate calling and ministry in the marketplace. . . . To honor God, to help people develop, to pursue excellence, to grow profitably is all part of God's work. . . . Our primary calling is a ministry to people, the people we work with and the people we serve. God's ultimate measure of our success, and the greatest testimony to His name, is the changed lives of people who are touched through our efforts. An environment that incites people to know God through His Son, Jesus Christ: this is the ultimate litmus test. This is the ultimate reason why growth, and the involvement of more and more people, is not an option for us, but a mandate. . . . We must recognize our responsibility to be stewards of all that God has provided for us.[13]

ServiceMaster's annual report each year lists the company's four objectives. They are: to honor God in all we do; to help people develop; to pursue excellence; to grow profitably. Pollard says that the first two statements define the company's goals; the latter two concern the means of reaching those goals.

Unusually sensitive environmental concerns come out of another company's commitment to biblical values. Applied Energy Services (AES), based in Arlington, Virginia, owns and operates several power plants throughout the United States. In 1986 it ranked twelfth in a list of the fastest-growing privately owned companies in America. One company officer asserted that they place a higher value on environmental protection than profit-making. "We tell our shareholders outright that our job is not to maximize the value of their shares. We're in business for other reasons."[14]

This commitment to environmentalism goes beyond state-of-the-art pollution control systems. In 1987 the company voluntarily spent $29,000 to relocate two 100-year-old oak trees at a plant site. They could, instead, have merely cut them down and replaced them with saplings, as the local county ordinances required.

Explicitly Christian in their company literature, the company incorporates Judeo-Christian values into every area of corporate life. Examples include:

1. Planting thousands of acres of trees in developing countries to offset the CO_2 greenhouse effect.
2. 35% of employees have stock options.
3. Offers to reduce the rate on contracts which have already been signed.
4. Operating committee meetings are open to all AES employees.

The company lists the following as the primary objective of the manager: the creation of an environment where other people can use their gifts and acquired skills to achieve the organization's objectives—stewardship of people.[15]

One final example comes from organized labor, perhaps an unexpected source. The Christian Labour Association of

Canada established its first locals in Ontario and British Columbia in 1952. It has since been certified by provincial labor relations boards in Ontario, British Columbia and Alberta (1963), Saskatchewan (1985), Manitoba (1986), the Yukon Territory (1987), and the federal labor relations board in 1978.

Unlike any other labor union in Canada, it bases its activities on the biblical teachings of social justice, cooperation, shared responsibility, and human dignity. Members do not have to be Christians (and often are not). But they must adhere to the CLAC's principles and values.

The impact of biblical values on this union's policies and practices is profound. Particularly noteworthy is the CLAC's rejection of the adversary relationship between management and labor.

> Labour relations are human relations, that is, they are first of all about people, people at work. Therefore, unions and the workers they represent find themselves at the cutting edge of life and human activity. It is here, where workers toil to produce the goods and services for society, that the values or beliefs by which they live from day to day come into focus. Unions must be prepared to grapple with these values, test and confront the beliefs that shape the thinking of workers and managers alike, and search for answers that will lead toward justice and harmony in the workplace.[16]

The CLAC is committed to offering voluntary binding arbitration prior to any strike action. In fact, since its inception in 1952 the union has struck only twice, both times because the owners refused binding arbitration. On the other hand, it believes that workers deserve more participation in decision-making than workers usually receive. This is based largely on the CLAC belief that people are created to be free beings, and that the corporation is a work *community* where all people are equally valued.

Owners and managers of companies will have to change their attitudes toward unions and realize that their employees are not merely cost factors, or commodities that must be bought on the labour market. Unions should be given the opportunity to be more than negotiators of contracts and the filers of grievances. Unions should be accepted as the spokesmen of labour, to be consulted and drawn into the planning and decision-making of the enterprise.[17]

These organizations provide us with startling proof that there is a Christian way of doing business. What is striking in each case is that the organization's policies and practices are both spoken and modeled by top management.

Ethical leadership, rather than elaborate ethical codes, is the key to running an organization, branch, or department to achieve desired values and practices. Coupled with setting the right example is a participative management style which allows employees to dialogue concerning corporate values and their implementation.

In contrast, some well-intentioned business people have made pathetic attempts at bringing Christianity into their organizations.

I think, for example, of the Buick dealer on the east side of Detroit who recently brought in evangelist Martha Jean Steinberg and choir from the Home of Love Church for a few hours of gospel singing and praying. Afterward, Steinberg invited fifty or so people in the showroom to pick out a new car. "We're going to pray a prayer of faith for all those who want cars," she said. "I'm saying to GMAC [GM's loan agency] that your credit will pass. Come back tomorrow and claim your car." Though many people pointed to the vehicles they wanted, no one came back the next day with a down payment.[18]

Now I want to address one of the most important economic principles in the Bible. It provides a foundation for the seven key values described above. It clarifies the ultimate mission of all economic activity. It suggests the ethical approach that should be paramount when ethical decisions must be made.

Out of this principle will come a number of related principles having to do with many facets of a Christian businessperson's life and activities. And it directly addresses the cornerstone of the private enterprise system—*the principle of private property rights.*

Several years ago I attended a political meeting hosted by a new Canadian political party called the Western Canada Concept. This short-lived party was committed to the separation of western Canada from the rest of the country to achieve greater economic prosperity for westerners. This outrageous goal made it impossible for most western Canadians to take the W.C.C. seriously, although many empathized with its feelings of alienation from the centers of power in Ontario and Quebec.

The meeting was attended by about 1,500 people, including many evangelical Christians. A number of the party's planks stirred considerable applause, none more than the call for private property rights to be entrenched in the Canadian constitution. Because the W.C.C. was committed to free enterprise as the only acceptable economic model, it saw such enshrinement as fundamental.

The W.C.C. was not alone in calling for the inclusion of private property in the constitution. Virtually all the provinces were urging the federal government of the day to do this. Many Christian voices were raised in support. In fact, the belief in the sacredness of private property rights is often cited as the reason why Christians tend to vote for private enterprise political parties.

Biblical Versus Capitalist Views of Private Property

Capitalism recognizes a relatively unrestricted right of private ownership of productive property (which can include land, buildings, technology, and so on). Owners are entitled to use, or even abuse, this property as they see fit. Among other things, the owner may withhold the services of his or her property unless he or she is remunerated adequately. For the vast majority of owners, the purpose of ownership is to maximize profits in the long run.[19]

What of the biblical perspective? To obtain it, we will have to plunge into the murky waters of Old Testament economic teaching.

In Egypt all land belonged to the Pharaoh (Gen. 47:20-26). In other ancient Eastern lands, the kings and temples owned large estates, although some land still rested in private lands. The feudal system prevailed among ancient Israel's neighbors—a piece of property was granted by the large landowner to an individual in return for the obligation to render certain services.

Although it was common throughout the Near East in the second millennium B.C., Israel did not experience the feudal system. Each Israelite family was apportioned a plot of land, to be maintained by the family forever (Lev. 25; Num. 27:1-11; 36:1-12). In a theological sense a feudal system existed, however; Yahweh[20] claimed ultimate ownership of the land, and gave Israelites dominion over their private acreages subject to a host of restrictions. "The land must not be sold permanently, because *the land is mine* and you are but aliens and my *tenants*" (Lev. 25:23, emphasis added).

These restrictions included:

1. Sabbatical Year and Jubilee. The sabbatical year, known by several different names (seventh year, Exod. 21:2; 23:11; sabbath of rest, a sabbath to the Lord, Lev. 25:4; year of release, Deut. 15:1-18), provided for the automatic release of Hebrew slaves. Every seventh year the land was to remain uncultivated and the vineyards and olive groves untended. Debts were to be canceled, and the poor lent whatever they needed.

   Jubilee was held every fiftieth year (after seven sabbaticals).

It was to consist of the return of any alienated land to its original owners or their heirs. Sowing, vintage, and harvest were prohibited (Lev. 25:8-17). Only land obtained by inheritance was permanent. Land obtained by other means reverted to the original family.

2. Redemption of the Land. If an Israelite was forced out of dire need to sell land, a near relative called the kinsman-redeemer (see Lev. 25:25, 47-49; Ruth 2:20, 3:9, 4:1-12; Jer. 32:6, 7) was to buy the land the kinsman had sold.

   The kinsman-redeemer had priority over all other purchasers. It was both his right and his obligation to purchase the property to retain it in the family.

3. Restricted Land Transfers. To the Israelite land was sacred, God being its ultimate Owner. The management of the family acreage was a significant moral responsibility. Even moving a landholder's boundary worker was a criminal act (Deut. 19:14). No free market in land, such as exists in Western nations today, was allowed.

   Thus an Israelite could only dispose of land in limited circumstances, primarily that of poverty (Lev. 25:25-26). The price of the land was also legislated. The value of the land was based on an estimate of the value of its yield until the next Jubilee. At that time the land reverted to the original owner or the heirs. In addition, the seller could renege on the deal at any time and repurchase the land if he could afford to do so, with the price calculated on the same basis (Lev. 25:24-28).

To summarize, all property belongs to God. *The Israelites were not to create a free market for productive property*. Rather, individual families were delegated the responsibility to manage God's "estate," over which the Lord retained ultimate ownership. *Land could not be sold for money which would be used for current consumption while possibly depriving future generations of their rightful inheritance.*

The Bible's Concern to Preserve the Family

Anticipating that some Israelites would fall into need and possibly have to sell their lands, the law provided such mechanisms as the kinsman-redeemer and the Jubilee to retain the land within the family or clan, and to eventually restore it to the original owners.

This concern for the well-being of the family unit both in the present and the future contrasts with that of Israel's neighbors. That the typical peasant was greatly oppressed is a consistent picture from ancient documents. Priests are shown as illegally invading the property of poor farmers and taking their crops. Rich people regularly exploited less-fortunate neighbors.

Among the most pitiable of the poor was the debtor. He and his family could be sold into slavery and remain in this state for life. A Sumerian proverb aptly brings home the oppressed state of many of the poor: "The strong man lives off what is paid for his strength, and the weak man off what is paid for his children."

Often the security demanded for a loan by the lender was the person of the debtor himself. This personal security might extend to his family and all his possessions as well. Thus, if the debtor failed to pay, he and his family often had to enter into the exclusive service of the creditor until the debt was discharged. Often the family was divided among various creditors.

It seems, then, that a key Old Testament principle is the preservation of the family unit. The large-scale accumulation of land by a few who would then be able to exploit the landless was avoided (see Isa. 5:8). Individual families were given a stake in the economic well-being of the nation. The economic security of future generations was thus assured. Economic balance and economic justice were achieved.

What is the relevance of this for modern Western families living in a free market economy? The accumulation of land and other productive capital is not to be an end in itself. It is a means to several important goals: the solidarity of the family unit, the economic security of future generations, and economic balance and justice in society generally.

Two important restrictions must be noted. First, private

holdings are not for our self-indulgent use. Second, exploitation must never mark economic dealings with others. Their families are as important as ours, and as deserving of economic justice and security.

Finally, economic activity must never contribute to breakdown within the family. This is a lesson many busy entrepreneurs and hard-driving professionals need to learn. Workaholism which robs the family of its deserved unity is wrong. Israelites took a full year off every seven from normal economic activity. Many business people have trouble taking off a weekend a month.

The Bible's Concern for All Needy People

But the obligation placed on private property owners by holding productive capital extends beyond their immediate families. There is no question that the right to own property is a legitimate biblical concept. Not only does the Pentateuch explicitly teach it, but the eighth commandment ("You shall not steal") reinforces it. I believe, however, that this right to own property is *subordinate* to the obligation to care for society's weaker members.

Three Old Testament teachings strongly suggest this further restriction on the self-centered use of private holdings.

1. The Poor Tithe (Deut. 14:22-23, 27-29). The Israelites organized years in cycles of seven, culminating in the Sabbatical Year. In each of those years a first tithe—a simple, proportional tax levied on each family's flocks, herds, and crops—was collected to support the Levitical system.

    But a second tithe was also required, for a different purpose. In years one, two, four, and five, a second tax in the form of a tithing of one's output was to be consumed by each family "in the presence of the Lord your God at the place he will choose as a dwelling for his Name" (Deut. 14:23). Rather than being placed at the disposal of the Levites, it was consumed by the producer in the context of worship in Jerusalem.

In years three and six, the second tithe was at the disposal not only of the Levites, but of the aliens, fatherless, and widows (all typically landless) who could not provide for themselves.

2. The Gleaning Laws (Lev. 19:9-10; Deut. 24:19-21; cf. Ruth 2:2-7, 15-17). Like the Poor Tithe, this means of redistribution, where the edges of the fields were to be left unharvested for the benefit of the poor and the alien, is sketchy in detail. No amount or percentage of the harvest is dictated. Presumably, generosity of the sort Boaz exhibited toward Ruth was to guide the reaper's decision.

3. The Capital Market (or the usury laws, Exod. 22:25; Lev. 25:35-37; Deut. 23:19-20). The law interfered in the financial capital market by forbidding the charging of interest on loans to poor brothers. Obviously this legislation provided a perfect disincentive to lending. Thus the law encouraged an openhanded attitude toward the needy despite there being no financial benefit from making the loan (Deut. 15:7-11).[21]

Redistribution of capital, then, is a normal response for those who accept biblical teaching. Those who had the opposite impulses, self-indulgently centering economic prosperity on themselves at the expense of the needy, were regularly condemned by the Old Testament prophets (see, for instance, Amos 8:4-8; Isa. 5:8-10, 10:1-3).

How Much Wealth Does the Bible Let Us Keep?

But just how far does this attitude toward our private holdings extend? Many of us prefer blueprints, specific percentages, explicit direction, so that we know when we've reached the magic number that pleases God. For this we will veer for a moment into the Gospels.

Luke has the most to say on the proper Christian attitude toward material possessions. Let me restrict myself to a brief overview of three motifs found in the gospel.

1. The call to renounce possessions totally. Again and again Luke 16 records Jesus as demanding renunciation of one's

possessions as a condition of discipleship.

This can be seen in the call of Simon Peter, James, and John (5:11), the call of Matthew (5:27-32), the story of the rich young ruler (18:18-23), Jesus' teaching on the cost of discipleship (14:33), the widow's pennies (21:1-4), the commissioning of the twelve (9:3), and the further commissioning of the seventy (10:1-4).

In nearly every case, Luke uses a particular Greek word (*panta*, abandonment) to underscore the renunciation of possessions and the totality of the call.

2. The dangers of wealth. At a time when Jews saw material blessing as a certain indication of God's favor, Jesus warns his followers to avoid the snare of wealth.

    References include woes pronounced on the rich (6:24-26), the parable of the sower (8:14; note that the seed is choked by life's riches and pleasures. In Mark's account the word is "choked," but in Luke it is the rich who are choked. They are seduced by their wealth), the parable of the rich fool (12:13-21), the rich man and Lazarus (16:19-31), and the famous camel going through the eye of the needle (18:24-30).

    Jesus' warnings in this last case were so severe that the Jews, accustomed to linking wealth with God's blessing, asked: "Who then can be saved?" Riches and faithful discipleship seemed now to be incompatible.

3. The right use of wealth, or the discipleship of possessions in the service of love. The outstanding example here is the story of Zacchaeus, the tax collector (19:1-10). Zacchaeus provides Luke's answer to two questions—how can the rich be saved, and how does one use one's possessions?

    Zacchaeus was a chief tax collector (he had underlings who collected taxes for him). He lived in prosperous Jericho. He is one rich man who did pass through the eye of a needle. He not only made restitution of ill-gotten gains according to rabbinic teaching (fourfold), but went much further, giving half of the remainder to the poor. This he did freely and joyfully. As such, he stands in bold contrast to the rich young ruler.

But isn't tithing sufficient? Do I not meet my obligations to redistribute my income when I have hit the traditional 10% mark?

Apparently such thinking is legalistic, at least in Luke's view. He records Jesus as saying that the Pharisees' scrupulous record of tithing was too easy (11:42a), that beyond this we must strive for justice and the love of God (11:42b).

In the next chapter Jesus urges his followers to seek his kingdom through, among other ways, selling all of their possessions and giving them to the poor (12:30-33). Obviously our attitude toward material life must be a sacrificial one. One's possessions are to be used for raising the downtrodden.

Am I then buying my way into the kingdom? We know better. The only entry to the kingdom of God is through saving faith in Christ (Eph. 2:8-9). One man who attempted the financial route to spiritual success found himself heading in a very different direction.

> When Simon (the Sorcerer) saw that the Spirit was given at the laying on of the apostles' hands, he offered them money and said, "Give me also this ability so that everyone on whom I lay my hands may receive the Holy Spirit." Peter answered, "May your money perish with you, because you thought you could buy the gift of God with money!" (Acts 8:18-20).

How is material life connected with our Christian walk, then? Obviously the amount of our wealth is not what matters. The widow's pennies counted for far more than the rich Jews' large offerings. A more likely explanation is that we as grateful believers place all our possessions, small or large, wholly at the Lord's disposal. We regard them as ultimately God's, to be used as God sees fit.

In accordance with Pentateuchal teaching, there is no room for self-indulgence. Rather, God blesses us with material resources as means to God's ends. These ends may take a variety of forms, but economic justice and stability are prominent among them. The implications of this for the businessperson contemplating personal and corporate responsibilities toward employees, customers, and society at large are highly suggestive.

The Key Biblical Principle: Justice

This study from both Testaments seems to point in the direction of *standards of justice as being the prominent avenue for making ethical decisions.*[22] Good consequences are definitely being sought, but not on a strictly cost versus benefit basis. Rather, all society's family units must be taken into consideration.

In ancient Israel, the majority did not win out at the unfortunate expense of the minority. In fact, in seeking justice the more well-to-do experienced significant personal loss, such as in the forgiving of legitimate debts and the return of alienated land. But this they did (or were supposed to do) joyfully—because they knew God ultimately owned their productive property. This recognition of God's rightful place at the head of all economic activity can be illustrated through two final Old Testament economic laws.

1. Fallow Year. As mentioned previously, both Sabbatical Year and Jubilee legislation provided for the land to be left fallow for the year. The crops that grew on their own were assigned to the poor for their personal benefit and, oddly enough, even to the wild animals (Exod. 23:10, 11; Lev. 25:5-17). All normal labor ceased for this year.
2. The Work-Leisure Decision. With comparable amounts of land and a zero return on financial capital, an Israelite got ahead by working hard. But significant restrictions were put on his labor. First, all men, women, children, servants, hired labor and animals were forbidden to work on the Sabbath (Exod. 20:8-10). Even the lighting of a fire was prohibited (Exod. 35:2-3). This amounted to 52 days per year of enforced leisure.

   In addition, the Israelites were to cease their work to celebrate the three great Pilgrimage Festivals—Passover (Exod. 12), Pentecost or Weeks (Deut. 16:9-12), Tabernacles or Booths (Exod. 23:16,17; 34:22,23)—plus New Year's (Num.

29:1-6), and the Day of Atonement (Lev. 23:27-32; Num. 29:7-11). This enforced leisure time was to be employed largely for spiritual pursuits.

Is economic activity and owning private property biblical? Definitely. Diligence in economic pursuits is encouraged over and over again. The right to private holdings is buttressed by no less prestigious legislation than the Ten Commandments.

Is the pursuit of profit illegitimate? Not at all. Nowhere is the accumulation of wealth denounced in Scripture. Material resources can even be a sign of God's favor (see Deut. 28).

Are profits an end in themselves, as the typical free enterprise position holds? Absolutely not. Material resources are means to further godly ends, not ends in themselves.

How does one use these resources? To seek justice and the love of God. Economic balance and justice were desired goals for ancient Israel. Paul suggests that such goals were still appropriate for believers in his time.

Our desire is not that others might be relieved while you are hard pressed, but that there might be equality. At the present time your plenty will supply what they need, so that in turn their plenty will supply what you need. Then there will be equality as it is written: "He that gathered much did not have too much, and he that gathered little did not have too little" (2 Cor. 8:13-15, quoting Exod. 16:18).

Holmes appears to be right in choosing justice and love as the key elements in constructing a Christian ethic. The biblical teachings we looked at suggest that individual human beings retain certain rights as God's image-bearers: to be treated with dignity and respect, to enjoy economic security within a stable family unit, and to be treated with justice. We must desire good consequences for all persons, and pursue justice so that these good ends are realized.

Human rights are a matter of justice, then. But love as well as justice must be our concern. Love will seek justice and concern itself with others' rights. But love will also go the second mile, deferring and even waiving some rights at times in loving service to others. Marriage and parenthood require this of both partners, and *they can teach us how to combine justice with love in other areas too* [emphasis added].[23]

One area where ethics must be explored is bankruptcy. I hope in my treatment of the issue I can model the exploration ethical dilemmas the businessperson faces.

I know I have not tied up all loose ends. I have placed the emphasis on standards of justice as a preeminent biblical principle. Individual moral rights and societal welfare also demand the Christian's attention, however.

Great spiritual sensitivity is necessary in deciding among the various approaches. Godly values may clash, leaving the decision-maker somehow to prioritize them according to the appropriate biblical principle. And beyond developing biblical discernment, the inevitable temptation to maximize one's own self-interests at the expense of others must be resisted.

Chapter 7
What the Bible Teaches About Debt

*Having lost its value, money may no longer be the root of
all evil: credit has taken its place.*
        —Dalton Camp, *Saturday Night Magazine*

Our task now is to determine the biblical teaching concerning debts and their repayment. The English word *debt*
appears infrequently in the Old Testament. The words *debt*
(1 Sam. 22:2; 2 Kings 4:7; Neh. 10:31), *debts* (Prov. 22:26),
and *debtor* (Ezek. 18:7) together appear only five times in
Strong's *Concordance.*

Three Hebrew words (or related derivatives) are represented by these five instances. In three cases debt is connected to the root idea of lending on interest or being a creditor.
The other two are one-time usages of more general words—
with the root idea of an open hand, and to tie or to owe, re-
spectively. In the New International Version of the Old Testament, the same words appear only a dozen times.

In the New Testament, the word *debt* is usually employed
figuratively as a picture of sin, such as in the phrase "Forgive
us our debts as we forgive our debtors." New Testament
writers knew of the very real problems debts, as well as the
great disparity between rich and poor caused in their times
(see Matt. 18:23-35; Luke 7:40-43; 16:1-9; Philemon 18). But
the specific economic teaching concerning debts is most fully developed in the Old Testament.

Fortunately, Old Testament passages do give us an excellent picture of the role of debt in the broader economy of God's people in ancient times. The challenge for us is once again to uncover the biblical principles which these ancient teachings imply.

What the Bible's View of Usury Teaches Us

A promising line of doctrine to pursue is the mostly ignored Old Testament one of interest (or usury) on loans. Combining this with the discussion of Pentateuchal economic teaching in Chapter 6 will provide us with much of what we need to evaluate the ethics of bankruptcy in Chapter 8.

The biblical use of the term *usury* corresponds to our modern word *interest* rather than to the notion of "excessive interest" to which we apply the term usury today. Few North Americans would ever question the morality of profiting from a loan at normal interest rates. Yet the Talmud quotes an ancient rabbi as saying: "It is better to sell your daughter into slavery than to borrow money on interest."

The biblical doctrine of usury rests primarily on three Pentateuchal texts: Exodus 22:25; Leviticus 25:35-37; and Deuteronomy 23:19-20. The first two prohibit loans of money or food with interest to a needy brother or sister or even a resident alien. The third text forbids taking interest from any person, rather than from just one's poor brother or sister. But it explicitly allows the lender to take interest from the foreigner.

Other Old Testament texts mentioning usury do not develop the doctrine further. But they do underline its importance. Psalm 15:5 characterizes a righteous man as one who, among other things, "lends his money without usury" (see also Ezekiel 18:8). Both Ezekiel 22:12 and Nehemiah 5:9-11 condemn lending money with interest, especially to the poor. And Ezekiel 18:13 lists the taking of interest among sins worthy of death.

It is important to keep in mind that charging interest was a common practice in the commercial Mesopotamian civilization of early biblical times. Babylonian contract tablets from the time of Hammurabi onward show payments of interest as a well-established custom. The Code of Hammurabi (1750 B.C.) sought to alleviate the economic burden of the poor. It did so by limiting interest rates to 20% for money loans, and 33 1/3% on grain. The term of the loan was from seedtime to harvest. Interest and principal were repaid in one lump sum at harvesttime.[1]

Despite such attempts, the debtor remained among the most pitiable of the poor in the Ancient East, and in later Greek and Roman societies as well.

The Old Testament prohibition, then, did not borrow from existing practice. It took an opposite position. While Hammurabi sought to limit interest rates, Israel's God forbade any interest.

To understand any Israelite institution, one must appreciate the all-embracing covenant of which it was a part. The covenant was a bond between the Lord and the Lord's chosen people. God took the sole initiative in establishing this bond—God's motivation was love (Deut. 7:8). The required response from Israel was also love. The multitude of commandments included in the covenant showed the way in which Israel's love for God and fellow human beings could be expressed.

The commands themselves touched upon what we today would call *sacred* matters (such as sacrifices) and *secular* ones (such as financial relationships and usury). The covenant made no such clear distinctions, of course. All of life was under the dominion of God. Israel was to be set apart from other cultures and to adopt a lifestyle worthy of God's holiness. This extended to the political economy of the land and the role of interest within that economy.

Usury and the Pentateuch

We will now explore the specific Pentateuchal teaching concerning the usury doctrine.

A. Exodus 22:25-27. If you lend to one of my people among you who is needy, do not be like a money lender; charge him no interest. If you take your neighbor's cloak as a pledge, return it to him by sunset, because his cloak is the only covering he has for his body. What else will he sleep in? When he cries out to me, I will hear, for I am compassionate (NIV).

1. *Context.* This passage is found in the context of the compassionate treatment of various oppressed groups: the sojourner or resident alien, the widow, the orphan and the poor. The alien lacked the protection of family and clan. The widow and orphan were ripe for oppression, lacking a male to look out for their interests. The poor were particularly vulnerable to exploitation and debt leading to bondage.

   Such concern for the poor is characteristic of the Old Testament (Deut. 15:4). The Law encouraged every conceivable act of generosity toward them: openhandedness (Deut. 15:8), gleanings in the field (Deut. 24:19), employment (Lev. 25:35), and the poor tithe (Deut. 14:28-29, 26:12). The Sabbatical Year and Jubilee were instituted with the poor in mind. Poor people were to be helped financially with interest-free loans, and no significant collateral was to be demanded.

2. *Pledges.* A fellow covenant-member was not to make another's poverty an opportunity for monetary gain. Thus, not only was interest forbidden, but only the most insignificant security was allowed. Forbidden as security were widow's clothing (Deut. 24:17), upper and lower millstones (Deut. 24:6), and the widow's ox (Job 24:3).

   The creditor could not even enter the debtor's house to receive the pledge; rather, he was to remain outside while the debtor brought him the pledge he deemed sufficient (Deut. 24:10-13). Clothing was a typical pledge (Exod. 22:26; compare Amos 2:8; Prov. 20:16; 27:13; Job 22:6).

   The choice of clothing was a common pledge. It had to be returned before sundown each day, which served two purposes. From the borrower's point of view, the loss of a cloak served as an annoying reminder of the debt that must be repaid (compare Gen. 38:12-26). For the lender, the sheer inconvenience of having to tramp over to the borrower's residence to pick it up every morning and drop it off every evening discouraged demanding a pledge at all.

To conclude, we find in this brief paragraph three reasons for the regulations concerning the oppressed. First, Israel was well aware of what life can be like as an alien (Exod. 22:21). Second, in a covenant community characterized by love ("my people," v. 25) exploitation could not be permitted. And third, since God is by nature compassionate (v. 27), compassion was demanded of God's people as well.

B. Leviticus 25:35-37. If one of your countrymen becomes poor and is unable to support himself among you, help him as you would an alien or a temporary resident, so that he can continue to live among you. Do not take interest of any kind from him, but fear your God, so that your countryman may continue to live among you. You must not lend him money at interest or sell him food at a profit.

1. *Context.* This second passage is found in a key chapter on economics that emphasizes God's sovereignty over the land, inalienable property rights, and the institution of the Jubilee. Verses 35-37 address one of the key problems in maintaining the proposed property system, the existence of usury.

   Whereas in Exodus 22:25 only money is mentioned and just the poor Israelite is singled out for attention, the Levitical command (perhaps in an attempt to plug loopholes being exploited by wily moneylenders) extends the loan to include food as well as money. It also includes the resident alien among receivers of compassionate treatment. In addition, verse 35, implicitly at least, *requires* that the needs of the poor be met ("support" or "sustain"; literally, "hold up").

2. *The resident alien.* Interestingly, beyond the fellow covenant members, the resident alien is singled out for equal treatment (compare Lev. 19:33-34; Deut. 24:14, 17). Sojourners tended to be poor since, as non-Israelites, they were excluded from ownership of land and had to hire themselves out as farmhands. We often find them included with other economically weak groups such as the widow and orphan

(Exod. 22:21-22). They are among eligible candidates for the poor tithe (Deut. 14:29), as well as interest-free loans.

To conclude, this passage supplements the earlier legislation in Exodus 22:25. Lenders were not to gain from any sort of loan. In verse 38 the compassion of God serves as a model for Israelites in dealing with their brother or sister or an alien.

C. Deuteronomy 23:19-20. Do not charge your brother interest, whether on money or food or anything else that may earn interest. You may charge a foreigner interest, but not a brother Israelite, so that the Lord your God may bless you.

1. Controversy. In the two passages considered thus far, the law has provided protection for the poor, both covenant members and dependent aliens. The Levitical passage seems to demand that the impoverished be helped with life-sustaining loans. But the law apparently did not object to lending with interest to people who enjoyed better economic circumstances.

Deuteronomy 23:19-20 materially changes our perception. An absolute ban on interest to any brother or sister is introduced, whether money, food, or any other loanable item. Was the Lawgiver expanding the scope of the usury prohibition? Certainly this was the understanding of later rabbis, and of the Christian church for at least sixteen centuries.[2] They interpreted the ban to apply to both consumer and investment loans.

Proponents of the view that a total ban was introduced cite at least two lines of evidence. The first involves the traditions recorded in rabbinic literature. In the thirty-second tractate of the Talmud (*Baba Metzia*), for instance, not only is the lending of money or foodstuffs at interest condemned—but even the "dust" of interest, meaning anything that smacked of usury. Examples include

a. Allowing a lender to live on the borrower's premises without rent or at reduced rent. In fact, if the borrower had lived there without paying rent prior to making the loan, the borrower must now be charged rent.

b. Sending gifts to a person prior to requesting a loan, or after granting a loan.

c. Words, in the form of valuable information or even in the form of a greeting to a lender who otherwise was never greeted.

The Talmud viewed usury as a denial of God. Interest-taking was connected with the gravest of sins, including idolatry, bloodshed, and robbery. Usurers were disqualified from being witnesses or judges. So were such "worthies" as the gambler, the tax-collector, extortioners, and herdsmen.

Usury was overwhelmingly rejected (although commercial pressures eventually led to some remarkable accommodations. For instance, a rabbi permitted a person to lend through a second party to a third, reasoning that the person who gave the gift was not the one who made the loan).

The second argument cited for a total ban in Deuteronomy is its emphasis on the word *brother*. For instance, Exodus 21:2 refers to a Hebrew slave. Deuteronomy 15:12 speaks of "your brother a Hebrew or Hebrewess" who is sold. Exodus 22:25 speaks of "my people." Deuteronomy 23:19 refers to "your brother" in the usury texts. Such examples are numerous. With respect to interest on loans, the emphasis on brotherhood, it is argued, includes the banning of interest-taking among all brothers and sisters.

2. *The Foreigner.* Before coming to any conclusion concerning the above arguments, one more "player" on the scene must be examined. "The foreigner" is distinguished from the resident alien in that he or she was not a permanent resident. As such, the foreigner did not enjoy the protection of law afforded the sojourner (Deut. 15:3; 23:20), nor could the foreigner participate in Israel's religious ceremonies (Exod. 12:43; Lev. 22:25).

The consensus of scholars is that the foreigner was in this case a traveling merchant.[3] For centuries Israel was almost exclusively a nation of peasants, while foreigners looked after commercial activities (compare Neh. 10:31; 13:15f.). Occasionally the word *Canaanite* is used simply to mean a trader (Zech. 14:21; Prov. 31:24). The law, in fact, seemed to connect the practice of interest-bearing loans to foreigners with domination of them.

In Deuteronomy 15:6, and again in 28:12, it is foretold that Israel would lend to many nations, but never borrow, thus ruling over them and never being subject to them.

Some fathers of the early church understood foreigner to

refer to an enemy. Ambrose, for instance, called the foreigner the notorious foe of God's people. "From him exact usury," he declared, "whom it would not be a curse to kill. Where there is the right of war, there also is the right of usury."[4]

A more likely interpretation, however, would view the evidence as pointing in the direction of certain kinds of legitimate commercial investments at interest.

3. *Conclusions.* Two possible interpretations can be considered. A more humanistic assumption is that a developing notion of brotherhood among the Israelites eventually led to a total ban on interest-bearing loans to one another, regardless of the purpose of the loan (relief of distress or investment opportunity). A strictly literal reading of the usury passages would lead to this conclusion, and this was the understanding of later rabbis and churchmen.

The other is that the covenant relationship required an attitude of love among covenant members that avoided exploitation in any form (such as taking permanent possession of another's property, permanent enslavement of a brother, certain pledges, interest). Wealth itself was a blessing from God (Deut. 8:11-18), but the accumulation of wealth was never to be at the cost of another's poverty.

Thus, the Israelite was permitted involvement in commercial affairs, which at that time meant dealing with a traveling merchant—but was not allowed to take advantage of a brother or sister. It would be difficult to construe a commercial relationship between two wealthy Israelites as one of taking advantage.

Interest, then, was not considered intrinsically evil, for it was allowed in the case of the foreigner. Within the Israelite economy it was considered evil in terms of the property system, and as a vehicle for oppression and exploitation. But where no such risk was present, commercial investments with interest were valid.

Despite the theme of mercy running through this legislation, Israelites appear largely to have ignored it. For instance, David's powerful guerrilla band was composed partially of displaced debtors (1 Sam. 22:2). We frequently witness prophetic denunciation of those who exploited their relationship with debtors (Amos 2:6-8; 4:1ff.; 6:4ff.).

Habakkuk warned these exploitative lenders that their avarice would "backfire" on them when debtors could finally take no more (Hab. 2:6f.). In post-exilic Judah, poor Jews were forced to use their own children as pledges to secure loans for the purpose of buying food (Neh. 5:1-13).

Is it any wonder, then, given the attitude of the typical moneylender that in the Wisdom literature of the Old Testament cosigning a loan was generally advised against? (Prov. 6:1-5; 11:15; 17:18; 22:26-27; 27:13).

Understanding Biblical Principles and Living Them Today

Once again we must look for the principles underlying this Old Testament legislation to apply it to a modern phenomenon such as bankruptcy. One scholar who has contributed much to our understanding of the process of recognizing biblical principles is Walter Kaiser. In *Toward an Exegetical Theology* he outlines the methods by which the principles underlying biblical teaching can be determined and applied in a contemporary context.

Kaiser defines *principlization* as follows:

> To "principlize" is to state the author's propositions, arguments, narrations, and illustrations in timeless abiding truths with special focus on the applications of those truths to the current needs of the church.[5]

Steps for uncovering biblical principles

The first step is to determine the subject of the biblical passage. This subject should reflect the major concern of the biblical author. To accurately describe the subject, it is necessary to determine what the biblical book as a whole is all about. Its major sections or parts, along with any arguments the author may be developing, must be noted. Then the special part the passage under study plays in the overall theme or argument of the larger material in which it is found must be examined.[6]

The economic teachings of the Pentateuch address the twin economic problems of scarce resources and insatiable

human desires. These inevitably led to exploitation and economic injustice. God's covenant community was to be characterized by holiness and love, which included economic
justice and stability, with an adequate living standard for all.
Paul may have had these principles in mind when he wrote
the Corinthians concerning generosity.

> Our desire is not that others might be relieved while you are
> hard pressed, but that there might be equality. At the present
> time your plenty will supply what you need so that in turn their
> plenty will supply what you need. Then there will be equality
> (2 Cor. 8:13-14).

The Levitical teaching on usury (Lev. 25:35-37) is found
in a key economic chapter dealing with the Sabbatical Year,
the Year of Jubilee, inalienable property rights, and so on. Its
broader context is the book of Leviticus itself, of course,
which emphasizes the holiness of God's people, set apart
from all other peoples.

Presumably the economic discussions in chapter 25 are a
contribution to this process of sanctification. The usury doctrine is then one aspect of holy living. This would fit not only
with the Levitical teaching, but with Pentateuchal economic
legislation as a whole.

Kaiser's next step is to find the emphasis of the text under
consideration, including important words and key terms.
Such words and terms may be identified by frequent occur-
rence.[7] Certainly in our Leviticus 25 example, the word *poor*
or other references to disadvantaged and economically dependent people occur repeatedly (v. 6: servants, hired
worker, alien; v. 14: do not take advantage; vv. 25, 35, 39, 47:
poor countrymen). God's constant command is that such
people are to be restored, treated mercifully, not exploited
or otherwise abused.

The third essential step is to determine the theology of the
text. This means identifying the permanent, abiding, and

doctrinal part of the passage. It is essential to examine the "informing theology" or "antecedent theology"—theology which has preceded the writing of the passage in question and influences the author's or editor's position.[8]

Exodus 22:25-27, the earliest reference to usury, no doubt influenced the shaping of Leviticus 25. As with the Levitical teaching on usury, so in Exodus the context of the usury doctrine is one of the compassionate treatment of various oppressed groups. It was noted earlier that throughout the Pentateuch a special compassion for the poor is found, with the ideal proclaimed in Deuteronomy 15:4: "There should be no poor among you."

Key principles are now readily apparent. Continued poverty is not compatible with a holy, loving covenant community. Poverty is an indication of lack of compassion and an invitation to exploitation. Lending to the poor with interest was a perfect example of these twin evils. As such it was forbidden. Where neither lack of compassion nor exploitation were an issue, then neither was usury.

This conclusion could be easily sustained—except for the apparent absolute prohibition of usury in Deuteronomy. But earlier in the chapter, I suggested that the argument for a total ban on usury for any sort of loan, whether to a rich or poor brother or sister, fails to take into account the identity of the foreigner (that is, a traveling merchant). It also ignores the fact that Palestine was a non-commercial society, where loans were normally needed in periods of financial crisis.

To understand a passage, one must first view it in its cultural, geographical, historical, economic, and religious settings or contexts. The early Christian church fathers totally overlooked the agricultural setting of the usury doctrine. They totally misunderstood the term *foreigner* in that context. Thus they concluded that usury was always wrong, except where it could be used to punish an enemy. They did not understand that the usury doctrine was an appropriate way of showing compassion toward poor people. They did not realize it contributed toward the broader principle of economic justice.

By Jesus' time, the Jewish financial system had become far more sophisticated. The days of small farmers holding inalienable property were long gone. Now many tenant farmers and day-laborers worked for wealthier Jewish and Gentile landholders on large estates.

Agriculture still dominated the economy. But Jews were much engaged in commercial life, especially in import/export activities. Evidence of this more advanced economy is seen in some of Jesus' teachings, including his parables.

Jesus' contribution to business principles

Despite the changed conditions, Jesus is true to the principles underlying the usury and other economic laws. Indeed, he goes beyond them. Consider, for instance, his admonition to creditors.

> And if you lend to those from whom you expect repayment, what credit is that to you? Even "sinners" lend to "sinners," expecting to be paid in full. But love your enemies, do good to them, and lend to them without expecting to get anything back. Then your reward will be great, and you will be sons of the Most High, because he is kind to the ungrateful and wicked (Luke 6:34-35).

> Give to the one who asks you, and do not turn way from one who wants to borrow from you (Matthew 5:42).

The passage in Luke is found in Luke's counterpart to Matthew's Sermon on the Mount. Luke 6:20-26 parallels the Beatitudes, describing life in the kingdom of God. In these verses we see a *reversal of the values of the world*. In 6:27-38 we find a second characteristic of kingdom life, *the law of love*.

Followers of Jesus were to be concerned with the welfare of others, even when met with hatred and abuse. As commentator G. B. Caird puts it, such love does not retaliate (vv. 27-31), seeks no reward (vv. 32-36), and is not judgmental (vv. 37-38).[9]

Jesus here exhorts his disciples to be sensitive to the needs of the poor regardless of their ability to repay. They must go beyond the best that the world can do. To lend only to those who can repay is too low a standard. It stresses security, not selfless love.[10]

The early church fathers shared Jesus' view of the relationship between creditor and debtor. Concerning the charging of interest on loans, for instance, the common perspective was that usury-taking was unacceptable for two reasons. It violated divine law. And it was contrary to Christian principles of love and mercy even in economic relationships. Consider, for instance, Basil the Great (A.D. 330-379).

> Tell me, do you expect to get money and profit out of the pauper? If he were in a position to add to your wealth, why should he come begging at your door? He came seeking an ally, and he found a foe. He was looking for medicine, and he lighted on poison. You ought to have comforted him in his distress, but in your attempt to grow fruit on the waste you are aggravating his necessity. Just as well might a physician go in to his patients, and instead of restoring them to health, rob them of the little strength they might have left.[11]

The consistent teaching of both Testaments, confirmed by the early church, is that compassion, mercy, and justice are to override purely economic concerns, such as loans. Christians are to be gracious to all, even debtors, whom we might legitimately treat in a less merciful manner.

While the Pentateuch restricted its teaching to members of the covenant community, Jesus appears to widen the application. He includes society at large (God does cause the rain to fall upon the just and the unjust). "I tell you, use worldly wealth to gain friends for yourselves, so that when it is gone, you will be welcomed into eternal dwellings" (Luke 16:9).

Chapter 8
The Ethics of Bankruptcy: A Biblical Perspective

In the "Our Father," Jesus is not simply recommending vaguely that we might pardon those who have bothered us or made us trouble, but tells us purely and simply to erase the debts of those who owe us money; which is to say, practice the Jubilee.
— *The Politics of Jesus*, John Howard Yoder

Is it biblical to claim bankruptcy? Christians differ strongly in their responses—but many are convinced that declaring bankruptcy is wrong.

Arguments Against Bankruptcy

Writing on business ethics, Mennonite author Ralph Hernley describes a situation in which the new owner of a newspaper learns he must pay a kickback of $500 to receive advertising from the county sheriff's office. Hernley's summary of the situation is revealing. "If the loss of the advertising income in the illustration above would have forced the owner into bankruptcy, he'd have needed to choose between *two unethical consequences*" [emphasis added].[1]

In Hernley's view, bankruptcy and paying kickbacks are apparently on the same moral plane.

We noted earlier the view of Albert Johnson. He sees no

place for bankruptcy with the possible exception of incredibly bad luck.

> Regardless of the leniency of the current bankruptcy law, the Christian finds no comfort in the Bible for taking such a step. Bankruptcy may be legal, but its morality is another question. This applies to both voluntary and involuntary bankruptcy. . . . I am aware that there are circumstances in which bankruptcy may be the only available option. The sudden death of the breadwinner in a family, an extended period of hospitalization, law-suits, and bills beyond the control of the family.
>
> But for many, bankruptcy comes up simply as a consequence of poor planning and bad judgment. Under such circumstances, I believe the obligation still remains to pay what is owed.[2]

Well-known personal finance consultant Larry Burkett leaves no doubt as to his opinion. In his workbook, *How to Manage Your Money*, he says,

> Is it scriptural to claim bankruptcy? It seem logical that if someone has incurred excessive debts and has a truly changed attitude, he should be able to start afresh, doesn't it? Read Psalm 37:21. How is the evil man described? . . . In *worldly terms*, to avoid debts seems logical. . . . When Christians transfer assets simply to avoid detachment by creditors, it reflects a *basic lack of trust and a deceitful attitude* [emphasis added].[3]

A hilarious illustration (purportedly true) of how some see bankruptcy as a godless act is provided by *The Wittenburg Door*. A Christian bookstore owner with debts to suppliers of $20,000 and assets of $3,000 is attempting to talk a major supplier out of pulling the plug on his business. He tries a spiritual "guilt trip." He ends three pages of rationalizations and excuses with the following pair of choices, asking the supplier to check one as his response:

> ☐ Okay, Mike . . . I understand your predicament. Perhaps we should have investigated your ministry's financial condition a little more thoroughly and not let your buyer run up the bill. In

any case, we've profited on any previously paid-for business you've sent our way, and the amount you now owe us is tax-deductible as a loss. . . . I believe you are sincere, and would not gain any personal pleasure in forcing either you or your ministry to legally declare bankruptcy. . . . We'll write off whatever your ministry owes us to His account.

☐ Your ministry OWES us that money, I don't care what Christ says, and we intend to sue you and your ministry. Go ahead and declare bankruptcy. Even if we don't get a penny and it COSTS us to sue, I'll have the satisfaction of your bankruptcy.

The Door was pleased to give this owner their coveted Green Weenie award, which is not recognition one wants to receive.[4]

The essence of the arguments against bankruptcy (with the exception of the last illustration) is that debts are lifelong obligations. Aside from very unusual circumstances, they must eventually be met, however long it takes to pay them off. Thus bankruptcy is a way to shirk one's Christian responsibility.

What the Bible Teaches About Debt

To properly evaluate this ethical controversy, it is important to be clear about what the Bible teaches concerning debt and the obligations borrowing places on the debtor. This we did in Chapter 7. We found that borrowers were obliged under normal circumstances to repay their debts.

This responsibility to meet obligations is particularly emphasized by a provision recorded in Leviticus 25:39. Here a debtor in default may go so far as to sell himself into slavery. The responsibility to repay one's debts was taken extremely seriously. However, the possibility of those debts being canceled (or debt-slaves released) was not ruled out. In fact, debtors were automatically relieved of their obligations every seventh year, whether or not they deserved compassion.

Wealth should generate compassion

Such compassion, including the setting aside of the legitimate rights of lenders, was typical of economic relationships in the Pentateuchal political economy. Let's review what we have learned about it.

If we were to choose one word to sum up economic life in the Pentateuch, it would be *stability*. Confronting us in the Law is a stable society with a guarantee of economic security to each family.

Wealth was viewed as a blessing from God (Deut. 8:11-18, 28). This blessing resulted from obedience and was based on God's compassion. The poor tithe, gleaning laws, and interest-free loans were tangible ways the Israelites could, in turn, show compassion for each other.

Beyond income-maintenance programs, the Law provided permanent mechanisms—such as the Sabbatical Year and Jubilee—to ensure that temporary misfortune barred no family from full participation in economic life.

Land was an inalienable right God had given each Israelite family. From it they were to derive their subsistence. The existence of wholesale usury could undermine the whole property system on which Israelite society was based. Thus this doctrine, along with others, supported a tribal system organized into clans and households, each owning property supposed to remain permanently in the family.

The Pentateuch reveals a closed economic system *impregnated by justice*. It was well suited to promote the larger goals of Jewish life. Israelite families were potentially freed from economic worries. They were able to devote themselves to the study of the Law and the worship and service of God.

Not every ethicist would place justice ahead of individual rights or societal benefit as a first consideration. Manuel Velasquez (whom I respect) reasons,

As we have seen, moral rights identify areas in which other people generally may not interfere even if they can show that they would derive greater benefits from such interference. Generally speaking, therefore, standards concerned with moral rights have greater weight than either utilitarian standards or standards of justice. And standards of justice are generally accorded greater weight than utilitarian considerations.[5]

Velasquez goes on to admit, however, that this "hierarchy" of ethical considerations does not always hold.

But these relationships hold only in general. If a certain action (or policy or institution) promises to generate sufficiently large social benefits or to prevent sufficiently large social harm, the enormity of these utilitarian consequences may justify limited infringements on the rights of some individuals. Moreover, sufficiently large social costs and benefits may also be significant enough to justify some departures from standards of justice; and the correction of large and widespread injustices may be important enough to justify limited infringements on some individual rights.[6]

An emphasis on societal implications in the Scriptures should not be surprising, given that Jewish thought and practice was much less individualistic than ours. As an Old Testament professor I once worked with put it, "We in the North American church liken ourselves to trees in a forest in our relationships with one another. The Jews saw themselves as leaves on a tree." The notion of a close relationship and mutual dependence dominated Jewish thinking.

Paul very much reflected this corporate perspective in his many illustrations of the church.

You are God's field, God's building (1 Cor. 3:9).

In him [Christ], you too are being built together to become a dwelling in which God lives by his Spirit (Eph. 2:22).

> From him the whole body, joined and held together by every supporting ligament, grows and builds itself up in love, as each part does its work (Eph. 4:16).

In this context of mutuality and interdependence, Paul instructed us,

> If you have any encouragement from being united with Christ, if any comfort from his love, if any fellowship with the Spirit, if any tenderness and compassion, then make my joy complete by being like-minded, having the same love, being one in spirit and purpose. Do nothing out of selfish ambition or vain conceit, but in humility consider others better than yourselves. Each of you should look not only to your own interests, but also to the interests of others (Phil. 2:1-4).

Income redistribution was to be the normal response of God's people (including creditors) in the Pentateuch. Likewise, acts of mercy and justice were to characterize followers of Christ in the New Testament, rather than an insistence upon one's rights.

But let us return to the specific economic teaching of the Old Testament. Velasquez suggests that we consider what kind of values are involved in choosing one kind of ethical action (say, standards of justice) over another (say, the protection of individual rights). We must then decide whether their importance and impact warrants choosing them.[7]

Within the community of the covenant people, economic justice and stability, compassionate treatment of the poor, and preservation of the family unit were put ahead of such strictly material concerns as repayment of debt. Deuteronomy 15:7-10 is particularly forceful:

> If there is a poor man among your brothers . . . do not be hardhearted or tightfisted toward your poor brother. Rather be open handed and freely lend him whatever he needs. *Be careful not to harbor this wicked thought: "The seventh year, the year for canceling debts, is near,"* so that you show ill will toward your needy

brother and give him nothing. He may then appeal to the LORD against you, and you will be found guilty of sin. Give generously to him and do so without a grudging heart; then because of this the LORD your God will bless you in all your work and in everything you put your hand to [emphasis added].

The Bible encourages some cancellation of debts

At this point, we may come to a tentative conclusion concerning the question of the ethics of bankruptcy. As I said, borrowers were obliged under normal circumstances to repay their debts. But the possibility of those debts being canceled was not ruled out.

Two points must be kept in mind. The cancellation of debts in the Old Testament was done at legislated intervals (Sabbatical and Jubilee years). Debtors' payment or nonpayment of debts was not in question. They may or may not have been culpable for their debt.

In addition, these borrowers were not big commercial investors. They were almost always farmers borrowing to preserve their means of making a living. They were covenant brothers—and they were poor. Quite often debt represented an obstacle to even a minimal standard of living as defined by that culture.

The Old Testament principle which can be legitimately extracted from the biblical model and applied to bankruptcy is that debt, while taken seriously, could be canceled to achieve some higher purpose—such as the preservation of the family. No noble goal is achieved when unscrupulous debtors are allowed to get off scot-free. But the Old Testament political economy did provide for the cancellation of debts as an act of mercy, with no stigma attached.

One last observation must be made concerning Old Testament legislation. It was not dependent on the goodwill of the lender. While lenders were to be merciful, debts were canceled whether they liked it or not. On the surface, such legislation appears naive, playing into the hands of wily borrowers prepared to take advantage of the system. Doubtless some did.

But the political economy of the Pentateuch reflected God's gracious covenant with his people. God was gracious and loving toward them. God expected in return their loving obedience, including the offering of grace and love to one another.

When God acted on behalf of God's people, blessing them materially, politically, militarily, and so on, all Israelites benefited. The undeserving were presumably dealt with by God. Similarly, individual Israelites were able to help the poor and raise them up to an adequate standard of living. If some were helped who did not deserve it, God respected the merciful heart of the lender, and rewarded the lender appropriately. No doubt any scheming debtor would inevitably receive a just reward as well.

Corporate social responsibility

Beyond obligations to creditors, another consideration which especially relates to business bankruptcies is corporate social responsibility. This is the responsibility business owners have to their employees, suppliers, customers, government, society generally, and in the case of Christians, to God.

As I said earlier, in capitalistic societies private property is viewed as the cornerstone of our economic system. North American free enterprise allows relatively unrestricted private ownership of land and other means of production. Owners of land and other capital can withhold use of these assets until they receive the price they desire. For most owners of capital, the long-term goal is maximizing profits.

No such purpose for private property is envisioned in the Pentateuch. God, concerned for economic stability and justice, gave each Israelite family a stake in the economic well-being of the country through *permanently held* land.

Pentateuchal legislation on inalienable property rights was concerned with safeguarding against poverty, preventing large-scale accumulation of land, and meeting the economic needs of future generations.

Such common free enterprise practices as mortgages and land speculation were condemned (see, for instance, Isa. 5:8). Lest there be any doubt as to who was ultimately in control, God gave an unambiguous command: "The land must not be sold permanently, *because the land is mine* and you are but aliens and my tenants" (Lev. 25:23).

Economist Carl Kreider carefully traces the implications of God's ultimate ownership of capital. He contrasts the communistic and capitalistic views of ownership of wealth with the Bible's and arrives at this conclusion: "The biblically significant question is what kind of stewardship can be devised which will enable us to be faithful in carrying out God's will for *his property*" [emphasis added].[8]

The significant point is that every aspect of a Christian's life, including ownership, is done "in the name of the Lord Jesus" (Col. 3:17). This suggests a total commitment to integrity of the sort that characterized Christ's own life on earth.

In the 5th century B.C., Malachi chastised God's people for falling short of this total commitment. Their failure was symbolized by the offering of sacrifices which did not meet the requirement that they bring the very best of their flocks and herds to the altar.

"When you bring blind animals for sacrifice, is that not wrong? When you sacrifice crippled or diseased animals, is that not wrong? Try offering them to your governor! Would he be pleased with you? Would he accept you?" says the Lord Almighty (Mal. 1:8).

Is Bankruptcy Ethical? No and Yes
We noted earlier that the major causes of commercial

bankruptcy include slipshod management and sloppy recordkeeping. Many entrepreneurs do not seek adequate education or advice in dealing with business problems.

Surely Christian businesspeople must recognize that such practices are indicative of the same lack of integrity which so disgusted Malachi (1:6-14). They must repent of anything less than a principled and totally professional approach to business ownership. It is the Lord Christ they are serving (Col. 3:23-25).

The forgiveness of a bankrupt's debts is possible. But Christian businesspeople must still see their business involvements as service in God's name—and act accordingly.

Often personal bankruptcies result from abuse of credit. There are Christians who take a strong position against any use of credit. One author and speaker claims that credit cannot be used wisely, only with differing degrees of foolishness. Seeing credit as a compromise to trusting God, he maintains that to be truly effective a Christian must be free financially. This is a remarkable statement, considering the many times God's people were urged to lend to the needy. How can it be blessed to lend (compassionately and generously) but evil to borrow?

The biblical doctrine of usury (which in the Old Testament means interest of any amount rather than excessive interest) does not entirely rule out the use of credit. Rather, it insists that another person's economic problems must not become an opportunity for an affluent lender to profit at a poor brother or sister's expense.

Certainly many of us North Americans do abuse credit, especially because the most expensive forms are also the most convenient. Credit-granting institutions determine our credit limits by looking at our total earnings and other debts. They assume we can use a large part of our total earnings to pay back these debts. But they do not take into consideration our overall financial objectives. This is fine for them, but not for us!

We Christians must begin by setting our financial objectives. We must keep in mind that we are not the ultimate owners of our wealth. Thus, the short- and long-range budgeting of our resources is the first step. We must plan our tithes and charitable giving, savings and investments, retirement plans, capital purchases, and so on. Questions concerning what is an appropriate lifestyle, given a Christian value system, must be answered.

Having set financial objectives, we can decide how much money we can afford to take out of current earnings to pay back debts without threatening our financial objectives. In this way we set our own credit limits. Bankruptcy due to abuse of credit is again a failure to recognize that we are but stewards of God's resources.

To summarize, the cancellation of debts the bankruptcy process permits is not necessarily immoral from a biblical point of view. Arguments to the contrary are usually based either on the idea of debts being lifelong obligations, or on the notion that most bankrupts do not deserve forgiveness because they are guilty of poor management or abuse of credit.

This study has tried to show that, while borrowers were expected to repay their debts in biblical times, all debts were supposed to be regularly canceled. Apparently the possibility of some debtors taking advantage of this was worth the risk. God would ensure that the compassionate lender would not in the long run be shortchanged.

Acts of mercy are never intended to encourage undisciplined lifestyles, of course. Sin does not abound so that grace might even more abound (Rom. 6:1-2). Christians must view economic life as part of their service to God, and in serving God we offer only "acceptable sacrifices."

Thus, the Christian who is petitioned into bankruptcy by creditors, or is thinking of voluntary bankruptcy, should carefully consider the alternatives which the law provides.

These include the proposal and the orderly payment of debts. Bankruptcy is sometimes permissible. But it is seldom desirable. It can affect lenders, suppliers, customers, and employees in adverse ways. It is not only the entrepreneur who bears the risk of participation in a business. Beyond these considerations, foregoing a discharge from debt by the courts in favor of trying to meet creditors' claims is a tremendous act of Christian witness.

Finally, what of Christian businesspeople who have, quite simply, "blown it"? Their management expertise was nonexistent, their decision-making illogical, their use of credit irresponsible. Now they find themselves hopelessly in debt, with restitution impossible. Does the Lord really expect us to forgive such a one as this? The authors consulted at the beginning of this study would, I believe, respond with a firm negative. But does the Bible provide specific guidance?

While modern forms of bankruptcy are not explicitly addressed by the Scriptures, the more general theme of poverty is discussed at length. Deuteronomy 15:4 proclaims the ideal: "There should be no poor among you." But poor there were, and God's Old Testament commands encouraged every conceivable act of compassion toward them.

The law was remarkably generous, in fact, because the Scriptures recognized that many bring misfortune on themselves. In the Wisdom literature, for instance, poverty is sometimes seen as the result of laziness (Prov. 6:6-11; 10:4; 20:4, 13; 24:30-34), the product of idle chatter (Prov. 14:23), resulting from worthless pursuits (Prov. 28:19), or caused by self-indulgent living (Prov. 21:17; 23:20-21).

Beyond this, some Old Testament passages point out that wealth and success are a blessing from God (Deut. 28:1-14), and that poverty can sometimes be understood as divine punishment. For instance, poverty is a threat used against those who break God's laws (Deut. 28:15-48; Lev. 26:14-26). Haggai and Malachi both interpret the poverty of Jews in their day this way.

Now this is what the Lord Almighty says: "Give careful thought to your ways. You have planted much, but have harvested little. You eat, but never have enough. . . . You earn wages, only to put them in a purse with holes in it" (Hagg. 1:6).

The Old Testament clearly recognizes, of course, that many people suffer from poverty through no fault of their own (Amos 5:10-12; Isa. 10:1-2). But it encourages liberality toward *all* the poor: openhandedness (Deut. 15:8), gleanings in the field (Deut. 24:19), employment (Lev. 25:35), and the poor tithe (Deut. 14:28-29; 26:12). The sabbatical year and Jubilee were instituted with the poor in mind (Leviticus 25). They were to be helped financially with interest-free loans, insignificant collateral, and forgiveness of debts.

While it is not stated explicitly, it would be consistent with Scripture generally that wrongdoers be expected to recognize their errors and mend their ways. God is both loving and holy; God is both parent and judge. Thus I conclude that any repentant sinner is a candidate for forgiveness, including repentant bankrupts.

I interviewed a Christian businessman who lost his investment in the business of a Christian brother who went bankrupt due to poor management. He had every right to be bitter. He not only lost his investment but, as an employee of the bankrupt firm, was without work for a year. He told me his only way out was to forgive and forget—without repayment. The owner had done a bad job and recovery was impossible. For the investor, the only adequate response he felt he could give was forgiveness.

Bankruptcy legislation was there to provide the bankrupt with a fresh start, free from a miserable and destructive life of being pursued constantly by creditors. And God's Spirit was there to allow the investor to forgive. That, too, is a tremendous act of Christian witness.

Conclusion

Bankruptcy is a troublesome and growing phenomenon. Church leaders must deal with it. Misfortune and reasonable risk-taking which backfired account for some economic failures. But many bankrupts are guilty of serious errors—poor management, abuse of credit, lack of financial controls, and so on.

Obviously the place to begin in dealing with bankruptcy is well before the fact. We counsel young people before marriage that they must build a solid relationship and avoid divorce. So too we should provide solid guidance to businesspeople and individuals concerning their stewardship of God's resources.

Individuals need to be reminded that bankruptcy has potentially devastating effects. It can seriously affect the financial well-being of suppliers, creditors, and employees. Its impact on one's feelings of self-worth can be enormous, as was seen in Chapter 2. A bankrupt's ability to contribute financially to the Lord's work will be severely hampered or completely curtailed. One's Christian witness may be hindered.

I have tried to show that bankruptcy is not inherently immoral. I think there are solid biblical grounds for forgiveness of debts without stigma. The principles underlying this have to do with economic justice and stability. They are not, however, meant to encourage undisciplined living.

Many people have been helped by bankruptcy legislation to get a fresh start in life. The result for some has been restoration to economic health and stability. Unfortunately, some Christians did not learn from the compassionate treatment they received. When bankruptcy led to new prosperity, they did not repay at least part of the old debts. They left their creditors "holding the bag" and centered their newfound prosperity on themselves.

This brings us to one last biblical principle: from everyone who has been given much, much will be demanded. If we receive merciful, compassionate treatment and are raised to new positions of affluence, we will now be expected to be merciful in turn. The leading religious figures of Jesus' day did not learn that lesson—and we know what Jesus said about them.

Notes

Introduction

1. Herman Loewen, "When I Went Broke," *The Marketplace*, May/June 1989, pp. 7-8.

2. Philip Marchand, "Dollar Sense," *Canadian Business*, Vol. 55, No. 11, November 1982, pp. 153-155.

3. Larry Burkett, *God's Principles for Operating a Business* (Dahlonega, GA: Christian Financial Concepts, 1982), audio cassette series, tape 1.

Chapter 1

1. *Power for Living*, July 3, 1983. A publication of Scripture Press Publications, Inc., Box 513, Glen Ellyn, IL 60137.

2. Albert J. Johnson, *A Christian's Guide to Family Finances* (Wheaton, IL: Victor Books, 1983), pp. 82, 85.

3. Gary D. Foster, "Think About It," *Bookstore Journal*, Vol. 16, No. 10, October 1983, p. 73.

4. *Statistical Abstract of the United States*, 1989. 109th edition, p. 527.

5. Roger LeRoy Miller, *Economic Issues for Consumers*, Sixth Edition (St. Paul: West Publishing Co., 1990), p. 358.

6. *Globe and Mail*, Toronto, ON. Monday, February 15, 1988, p. B1.

7. *Globe and Mail*, Toronto, Aug. 12, 1985, p. B1.

8. Robert Hartzler, "Where Was God (when the farm failed)," *Mennonite Brethren Herald*, January 24, 1986, pp. 8-9.

9. Johnson, *Family Finances*, p. 81.

10. *The Vancouver Sun*. Friday, July 15, 1983, p. B5.

11. Roger Tassé, John D. Honsberger, Pierre Carignana and Raymond A. Landry, *Report of the Study Committee on Bankruptcy and Insolvency Legislation* (Ottawa: Information Canada 1970), pp. 55-56. See also Larry Huizingh and Bernard Wilson, "Getting the (Bankruptcy) Act Together," *Canadian Banker and ICB Review*, Volume 89, Number 1, February 1982, p. 31: "The removal of the stigma that was associated with bankruptcy as recently as two decades ago has made bankruptcy easy and has led to some abuses. Certain individuals look to bankruptcy as a simple cure for their financial difficulties."

Chapter 2

1. Preston Manning, lecture entitled, "Good News for Bad Times,"

Regent College, Vancouver, B.C., January, 1983.

2. Christina Toth, "Market Threatens to Bury Growers," *Abbotsford, Sumas & Matsqui News*, Wednesday, May 16, 1990, p. A2.

3. Walter O. Meloon, "On the Edge of Bankruptcy," *Decision*, April 1986, pp. 10-11.

4. "Success Religion," *Testament*, a CBC radio series about the religious experience of today, produced by Don Mowatt and Katherine Carolan, July 3, 1983.

5. Gordon D. Fee, "The 'Alien' Gospel of Prosperity," *Presbyterian Communique*, April-June 1981, pp. 21-22.

6. Ulrich Schaffer, *Greater Than Our Hearts* (New York: Harper and Row, 1981), p. 33.

7. Manning, "Good News."

8. Milt Kuyers, "Do Christ and Business Mix?" *The Banner*, May 14, 1990, p. 9. See also Robert V. Thompson, *Unemployed*, Downer's Grove, IL: IVP, 1983, p. 5. Thompson is a Baptist pastor who leads an unemployment support and resource group meeting weekly at his church.

9. For an interesting parallel description of the effects of unemployment see Esther Krystal, Marsha Moran-Sackett, Sylvia V. Thompson, and Lucile Cantoni, "Serving the Unemployed," *Social Casework*, 1981 (Feb.), Vol. 64(2), pp. 67-76. The authors note that unemployed individuals experience major bereavement reactions.

10. Mike Grenby, "There is life after bankruptcy," *Abbotsford-Clearbrook Times*, Wednesday, July 27, 1988, p. 24.

Chapter 3

1. Graham Cunningham, "Blame bad management, not high interest rates," *Financial Times of Canada*, April 26, 1982, p. 23.

2. Michael Ryval, "Is Your Business Going for Broke?" *The Financial Post Magazine*, October 31, 1981, p. 40.

3. Bernard Wilson, "Spotting the Danger Signals," *The Canadian Banker and ICB Review*, Vol. 86, No. 5, October 1979, p. 32. See further: John D. Honsberger, "Corporate Failure Can Be Predicted," *CA Magazine*, June 1979, pp. 30-32.

4. Larry E. Greiner, "Evolution and Revolution as Organizations Grow," *Harvard Business Review*, July/August 1972. Reprinted in *The Organization Game*, Robert H. Miles and W. Alan Randolph, editors. Glenview, IL: Scott, Foresman and Co., 1979, pp. 64-73.

5. Greiner's views are backed up over and over again in surveys of failed companies. For example a study by Prof. Russell Knight of the University of Western Ontario found that lack of management experience leads to mismanagement. "The primary problems of small business are

caused by a lack of management expertise." Symptoms are low sales, high inventories, large operating expenses, lack of control over receivables (poor credit-granting practices and inability to collect), and cash flow. See Ken Romain, "Lack of management skills greases skid to bankruptcy," *Globe and Mail*, Friday, May 29, 1987, p. C12.

6. Messer, "Canadian Bankruptcies," p. 32.

7. Ryval, "Going for Broke," p. 42.

8. Jack Taylor, "Business Failure: Why It Happens, and How to Avoid It Through Planning," *Small Business Review*, Vol. 3, No. 1, November 1982, p. 2.

9. Rea Godbold, "Life on the Receiving End," *Canadian Business*, Vol. 55, No. 6, June 1982, p. 86.

10. Tracy Le May, "Management: The Key to Survival," *Financial Times*, April 26, 1982, pp. B10-B11. For another excellent article on financial management see George Fox, "Looking Out for the Seven Early Warning Signs," *Credit and Financial Management*, Vol. 83, No. 11, December 1981, pp. 30-32.

11. Ed Harris, "Straight Talk About Why Businesses Fail—And How They Can Be Saved," *Canadian Business*, Vol. 53, No. 7, July 1980, p. 160.

12. Cheryl Hawkes, "Bankruptcy: The Best Medicine," *Canadian Business*, Vol. 54, No. 12, December 1981, p. 123. See also Mary-Margaret Wantuck, "Keeping a Small Business Afloat," *Nation's Business*, April 1985, p. 53.

13. Ryval, "Going for Broke," p. 40.

14. By way of contrast, the Christian Farmers Federation of Ontario defended the banks. In a statement issued in mid-1987 it stated: "Those of us who used demand loans during that period of high interest understood the arrangements being made. . . . We believe the high cost of borrowing to be wrong but we do not accuse the banks of wrongdoing." It called upon financial institutions "to walk the extra mile" with farm families who were in trouble. See "Christian farmers turn the other cheek," *Christian Week*, Winnipeg, MB, August 18, 1987, p. 1.

15. Meloon, "On the Edge of Bankruptcy," p. 10.

16. John Alexander Haskett, "It's Your Money," *CGA Magazine*, Volume 14, No. 6, June/July 1980, p. 24.

17. J. W. Brighton, J. A. Connidis, *Consumer Bankrupts in Canada* (Ottawa: Minister of Supply and Services Canada, 1982), p. 34.

18. Otto Griedrich, "The American Way of Debt," *Time Magazine*, May 31, 1982, p. 47.

19. Source: Statistics Canada. For an excellent discussion of the use of credit by age, income, class, and attitude toward debt, see Kathleen H. Brown, *Personal Finance for Canadians*, 3rd edition (Scarborough, Ontario: Prentice-Hall Canada) 1988, pp. 316-325.

20. Brighton and Connidis, p. 19.

21. Ibid., pp. 23-25.

22. Ibid., p. 31.

23. Ibid., p. 51.

24. Ibid., p. 39.

25. Ibid., p. 33.

26. Ibid., Summary.

Chapter 4

1. Carl Roebuck, *The World of Ancient Times* (New York: Charles Scribner's Sons, 1966), p. 439-440.

2. Tassé, et al., *Report on Bankruptcy*, p. 5.

3. Roebuck, p. 445.

4. John A. Willes, *Contemporary Canadian Business Law* (Toronto: McGraw-Hill Ryerson, 1981), p. 711.

5. Tassé, pp. 7-8, 10.

6. Tassé, pp. 10-11.

7. Bernard Wilson, "The Last Resort," *The Canadian Banker & ICB Review*, Vol. 87, No. 3, June 1980, pp. 20-22; Willes, pp. 714-719; Tassé, pp. 27-31.

8. At present, the OPD is available in the provinces of British Columbia, Alberta, Saskatchewan, Manitoba, Prince Edward Island, and Nova Scotia. Similar mechanisms exist in Ontario and Quebec.

9. Michael Ryval, "Is Your Business Going for Broke?" *The Financial Post Magazine*, October 31, 1981, pp. 44-45; Bill Annett, "Corporate Insolvency and the CGA," *CGA Magazine*, Vol. 17, No. 5, May 1983, pp. 17-22; Bernard Wilson, "A Customer Saved Is a Customer Gained," *The Canadian Banker & ICB Review*, Vol. 86, No. 6, December 1979, p. 13. Bill Annett, "Bankruptcy or Born-Again Business?" *B.C. Business*, Vol. 10, No. 7, September 1982, pp. 25-30; Bernard R. Wilson, "The Creditor's Crunch," *Canadian Business*, Vol. 56, No. 4, March 1983, pp. 113-117.

10. John Jude Moran, *Practical Business Law* (Englewood Cliffs, NJ: Prentice-Hall, Inc., 1985) pp. 245-257; Jordan L. Paust, Robert D. Upp, John E. H. Sherry, *Business Law*, Fourth Edition (St. Paul: West Publishing Co., 1984), pp. 692-697; Mary-Margaret Wantuck, "A Better Balance in Bankruptcy Law," *Nation's Business*, April, 1985, pp. 50-53.

Chapter 5

1. *The Sun,* Vancouver, British Columbia, January 30, 1989, p. A4.

2. Oliver F. Williams and John W. Houck. *Full Value* (San Francisco: Harper & Row, Publishers, 1978), pp. 5-6.

3. *The Province*, Vancouver, British Columbia, August 25, 1987, p. 19.

4. "Jesus in the Office," *The Banner*, May 14, 1990, p. 7.

5. *Wall Street Journal*, New York, a Wall Street Journal/Gallup Survey entitled "Ethics in America," October 31 through November 3, 1983.

6. Clare Ansberry, "For These M.B.A.'s, Class Became Exercise in Corporate Espionage," *The Wall Street Journal*, Tuesday, March 22, 1988, p.37.

7. "Jesus in the Office," p. 7.

8. Robert C. Solomon and Kristine Hanson. *It's Good Business* (New York: Atheneum, 1985), pp. xi-xii.

9. Tad Tuleja. *Beyond the Bottom Line* (New York: Facts on File Publications, 1985).

10. *The Sun*, Vancouver, British Columbia, January 4, 1988, p. B1.

11. William J. Krutza, "The Nearsighted Ethics of Christian Businessmen," *Eternity*, September 1976, p. 15.

12. Ibid., p. 16.

13. Kuyers, "Do Christ and Business Mix?" pp. 8-9.

14. "Jimmy Pattison: The Man Behind Expo '86," *Faith Today*, September 1986, p. 31.

15. Manuel G. Velasquez. *Business Ethics*, Second Edition (Englewood Cliffs, NJ: Prentice Hall, 1988), p. 10.

16. Robert C. Solomon and Kristine R. Hanson. *Above the Bottom Line: An Introduction to Business Ethics* (New York: Harcourt Brace Jovanovich, Inc., 1983), p. 9.

17. *Journal of Business Ethics* (Dordrecht: Kluwer Academic Publishers). See also Rogene A. Buchholz. *Fundamental Concepts and Problems in Business Ethics*. (Englewood Cliffs, NJ: Prentice Hall, 1989), pp. 2-3.

18. William C. Frederick, Keith Davis, and James E. Post. *Business and Society: Corporate Strategy, Public Policy, Ethics*. 6th edition (New York: McGraw Hill Book Company, 1988), p. 52.

19. Holmes, *Ethics*, p. 10. See also John B. Matthews, Kenneth E. Goodpaster, and Laura L. Nash. *Policies and Persons* (New York: McGraw-Hill Book Company, 1985), p. xii; Velasquez, *Business Ethics*, pp. 10ff.

20. Dutch scholar Sybren Tijmstra, for instance, views ethics as "the human striving for happiness, consisting of and/or leading to thoughts concerned with good and wrong." See Cees van Dam and Lund Stallaent, eds. *Trends in Business Ethics*. (Boston: Kluwer Boston Inc., 1978), p. 160.

21. Leonard James Brooks, "Business Ethics: Directions for the 1990's," *Canadian Business Review*, Spring 1990, p. 38.

22. Kirk O. Hanson. "Ethics and Business: A Progress Report," *Stanford GSB*, Spring 1983, p. 11.

23. J. J. C. Smart, "Extreme and Restricted Utilitarianism," in *Approaches to Ethics*, 2nd edition, ed. W. T. Jones et al. (NY: McGraw Hill, 1969), pp. 625-633.

24. Solomon and Hanson. *It's Good Business*, pp. 5-6.

25. *Faith Today*, September 1986, p. 31.

26. John De Mont, "Tapping a market: swimsuit magazines are earning big profits," *Maclean's*, February 20, 1989, p. 28.

27. Harold Lindsell. *Free Enterprise: A Judeo-Christian Defense*. (Wheaton, IL: Tyndale House Publishers, Inc., 1982), p. 75. See my book review of Lindsell in *CRUX*, Vol. XIX, No. 2, June 1983, pp. 30-31.

28. Betty Trott. "Ethics and the Executive: What Works Is Not Always Enough," *Executive*, April 1983, p. 64.

29. Hanson, "Ethics and Business," *Stanford GSB*, p. 11.

30. Velasquez, *Business Ethics*, pp. 72-73.

31. Holmes, *Ethics*, pp. 44-45. Many writers have attempted to outline an approach to measurement of utility (or benefit) in making business decisions. See, for instance, Walter Kiechel III, "Unfuzzing Ethics for Managers," *Fortune*, November 23, 1987, pp. 232-234, although Kiechel recommends that the process should incorporate some standard of justice.

32. See Velasquez, *Business Ethics*, pp. 81-90, for an excellent overview of the concept of rights.

33. Ibid., pp. 90-99.

34. Holmes, *Ethics*, pp. 79-89.

35. Frederick et al., *Business and Society*, p. 61.

36. R. Laird Harris, editor. *Theological Wordbook of the Old Testament*, Vol. 2 (Chicago: Moody Press, 1980), pp. 2443-2444.

37. I am indebted to Prof. Elmer Martens of the Mennonite Biblical Seminary in Fresno, Calif., for this material which was included in a course he gave at Regent College, Vancouver, B.C., in 1988. See E. A. Martens. *Jeremiah*. (Scottdale, PA: Herald Press, 1986).

38. Holmes, *Ethics*, p. 50.

39. Ibid., p. 52.

40. Russell Kelly. *Pattison: Portrait of a Capitalist Superstar*. (Vancouver, B.C.: New Star Books Ltd., 1986), pp. 45-46.

41. Matthews et al., *Policies and Persons*, p. 518.

Chapter 6

1. See, for instance, Tuleja, *Beyond the Bottom Line*, p. 25: "My own attachment to enlightened self-interest is evident. Yet I appreciate the common-sense value of utilitarianism, especially to business people, and in this book I will be using an ethical model that combines elements of the Benthamite (i.e., utilitarian) and Kantian (i.e., categorical imperative) systems." See also Thomas M. Garrett and Richard J. Klonoski, *Business Ethics*, 2nd ed. (Englewood Cliffs, NJ: Prentice-Hall, Inc., 1986), pp. 13-14: "Many contemporary writers on ethics tend to focus either on consequences or on intentions. While some ethical problems are clearly best attacked from the

perspective of consequences and others most fruitfully analyzed by examining intentions, the vast majority of ethical dilemmas encountered in business require *both* the weighing of consequences and the scrutiny of intent."

2. Laura L. Nash. "Ethics without the sermon," *Harvard Business Review*, November-December 1981, pp. 79-90.

3. Walter Kiechel III, "Unfuzzing Ethics for Managers," pp. 232-234.

4. Frederick et al., *Business and Society*, pp. 62-64.

5. Garrett, *Business Ethics*, pp. 1-2.

6. Holmes, *Ethics*, p. 51.

7. Ibid., pp. 51-52.

8. Harold L. Johnson, "Can the Businessman Apply Christianity?" *Harvard Business Review: The Business of Ethics and Business*. Special collection of classic articles copyright various years from 1957 to 1986, volume no. 11043, p. 116.

9. Reasons for judgment of the Honourable Mr. Justice Bouck, in the Supreme Court of British Columbia, between the Board of School Trustees of School District 34 (Abbotsford) and John and Ilze Shewan, January 30, 1986, p. 34.

10. Williams and Houck, *Full Value*, pp. 24-38.

11. Gordon Brockhouse, "Good Works: When business and religion mix, tolerance is the golden rule," *Office Management and Automation*, Vol. 4, No. 1, January 1988, pp. 37-38.

12. Edwin Darby, "ServiceMaster Cleans Up in a Big Way," *Commerce*, February 1985.

13. C. William Pollard, "Work: A Calling or Curse," unpublished paper, no date.

14. "Positive Power," *Money Matters*, Vol. 5, No. 1, Spring 1988.

15. Taken from materials provided by company president Dennis W. Bakke in an address to a Christian College Coalition conference entitled "Business in the Christian College Classroom," Wheaton College, May 23-27, 1988.

16. Ed Grootenboer, *About Work and Unions*. (Toronto: Christian Labour Association of Canada, 1984), pp. 5-6.

17. Ibid., p. 11.

18. "Jesus in the Office," p. 7.

19. See the excellent discussion of capitalism in Robert L. Heilbroner, *The Making of Economic Society*, 6th edition (Englewood Cliffs, NJ: Prentice-Hall, Inc., 1980), ch. 14.

20. "Yahweh" is the more accurate rendering of the Hebrew name for God, better known (although less correctly) as "Jehovah," usually written as LORD in modern English Bibles.

21. John R. Sutherland, "Usury: God's Forgotten Doctrine," *CRUX*, Vol. XVIII, No. 1, March 1982, pp. 9-14.

22. See the excellent discussion on doing justice in business in Richard C. Chewning, John W. Eby, and Shirley J. Roels, *Business Through the Eyes of Faith* (San Francisco: Harper & Row, 1990).

23. Holmes, *Ethics*, p. 89.

Chapter 7

1. James B. Pritchard, *Ancient Near Eastern Texts* (Princeton University Press, 1955), pp. 163ff.

2. See, for instance, *Encyclopedia Judaica* (Jerusalem: Keter Publishing House, 1971), pp. 27-31; F. L. Cross and E. A. Livingstone, "Usury," *The Oxford Dictionary of the Christian Church*, 2nd ed. (London: Oxford University Press, 1974), p. 1420.

3. G. Von Rad, *Deuteronomy* (Philadelphia: Westminster Press, 1966), pp. 19-20.

4. Benjamin Nelson, *The Idea of Usury* (Chicago: University of Chicago Press, 1969), pp. 3-4.

5. Walter C. Kaiser, *Toward an Exegetical Theology* (Grand Rapids: Baker Book House, 1981), p. 152.

6. Ibid., pp. 152-153.

7. Ibid., p. 155.

8. Ibid., pp. 134-140, 161-162.

9. G. B. Caird, *Saint Luke: The Pelican New Testament Commentaries* (Harmondsworth, Middlesex, England: Penguin Books, 1963), pp. 100-105.

10. Leon Morris, *The Gospel According to St. Luke* (Grand Rapids: Wm. B. Eerdmans, 1974), pp. 130-131.

11. Philip Schaff and Henry Wace, *The Nicene and Post-Nicene Fathers*, Second Series, vol. 8 (Grand Rapids: Wm. B. Eerdmans, reprint), pp. xlvii-xlix.

Chapter 8

1. J. Daniel Hess, *Ethics in Business and Labour* (Scottdale, PA: Herald Press, 1977), p. 7.

2. Johnson, *Family Finances*, pp. 81, 83-84.

3. Larry Burkett, *How to Manage Your Money* (Chicago: Moody Press, 1971), p. 27. See also Burkett, *Your Finances in Changing Times* (Campus Crusade for Christ, Inc., 1971), pp. 65-66.

4. "Loser of the Month," *The Wittenburg Door*, No. 51, October/November 1979, p. 26.

5. Velasquez, *Business Ethics*, p. 117.

6. Ibid., p. 117.

7. Ibid., p. 118.

8. Carl Kreider, *The Christian Entrepreneur* (Scottdale, PA: Herald Press, 1980), p. 41.

Bibliography

Alexander, John. *Your Money or Your Life*. San Francisco: Harper
and Row, 1986.

Annett, Bill. "Bankruptcy or Born-Again Business." *B.C. Business*,
Vol. 10, No. 7, September 1982.

Annett, Bill. "Corporate Insolvency and the CGA." *CGA Magazine*,
Vol. 17, No. 5, May 1983.

Barron, Bruce. *The Health and Wealth Gospel*. Downers Grove, IL:
InterVarsity Press, 1987.

Blackburn, Tom. *Christian Business Ethics*. Chicago: Fides/Claretian,
1981.

Blanchard, Kenneth H., and Peale, Norman Vincent. *The Power of
Ethical Management*. New York: W. Morrow, 1988.

Bowie, Norman. *Business Ethics*. Englewood Cliffs, NJ: Prentice-
Hall, Inc., 1982.

Brady, F. Neil. "Practical Formalism: A New Methodological Proposal for Business Ethics." *Journal of Business Ethics*, Vol. 7, No.
3, March, 1988.

Brighton, J. W., and Connidis, J. A. *Consumer Bankrupts in Canada*.
Ottawa: Minister of Supply and Services Canada, 1982.

Brockhouse, Gordon. "Good Works: When Business and Religion
Mix, Tolerance Is the Golden Rule." *Office Management and
Automation*, Vol. 4, No. 1, January 1988, pp. 37-38.

Brown, Kathleen H. *Personal Finance for Canadians*. Scarborough,
ON: Prentice-Hall Canada, Inc., 1988.

Buchholz, Rogene A. *Fundamental Concepts and Problems in Business
Ethics*. Englewood Cliffs, NJ: Prentice-Hall, Inc., 1989.

Burkett, Larry. *God's Principles for Operating a Business*. Dahlonega,
GA: Christian Financial Concepts, 1982, Audio cassette series, tape 1.

Burkett, Larry. *How to Manage Your Money*. Chicago: Moody Press,
1971.

Burkett, Larry. *Your Finances in Changing Times*. Campus Crusade
for Christ, Inc., 1971.

Caird, G. B. *Saint Luke: The Pelican New Testament Commentaries*.
Harmondsworth, Middlesex, England: Penguin Books, 1963.

Chewning, Richard C.; Eby, John W.; and Roels, Shirley J. *Business

Through the Eyes of Faith. San Francisco: Harper & Row, Publishers, 1990.

"Christian Farmers Turn the Other Cheek." *Christian Week*. Winnipeg, MB, August 18, 1987.

Cooper, Jeanne Duban. "Bankruptcy Loses Stigma as Debtors' Last Resort," *Newsday*. October 1, 1990, p. 4 (Business).

Cross, F. L., and Livingston, E. A. "Usury." *The Oxford Dictionary of the Christian Church*, 2nd ed. London: Oxford University Press, 1974.

Crouch, Gregory. "The Boom in Bankruptcies," *The Los Angeles Times*. April 16, 1990. p. 6D.

Cunningham, Graham. "Blame Bad Management, Not High Interest Rates." *Financial Times of Canada*. April 26, 1982.

Darby, Edwin. "ServiceMaster Cleans Up." *Commerce*. February, 1985.

De George, Richard T. *Business Ethics*. New York: Macmillan, 1982.

De Mont, John. "Tapping a Market: Swimsuit Magazines Are Earning Big Profits." *Maclean's*. February 20, 1989.

Donaldson, Thomas, and Werhane, Patricia H., eds. *Ethical Issues in Business*. Englewood Cliffs, NJ: Prentice-Hall, Inc., 1979.

Ellul, Jacques. *Money and Power*. Downers Grove, IL: InterVarsity Press, 1984.

Encyclopedia Judaica. Jerusalem: Keter Publishing House, 1971.

Fee, Gordon D. "The 'Alien' Gospel of Prosperity." *Presbyterian Communique*. April-June, 1981.

Forell, George W., and Lazereth, William H., eds. *Corporation Ethics: The Quest for Moral Authority*. Philadelphia: Fortress Press, 1980.

Foster, Gary D. "Think About It." *Bookstore Journal*, Vol. 16, No. 10, October, 1983.

Fox, George. "Looking Out for the Seven Early Warning Signs." *Credit and Financial Management*, Vol. 83, No. 11, December 1981.

Frankena, William. *Ethics*. Englewood Cliffs, NJ: Prentice-Hall, Inc., 1973.

Frederick, William C.; Davis, Keith; and Post, James E. *Business and Society: Corporate Strategy, Public Policy, Ethics*, 6th ed. New York: McGraw-Hill Book Company, 1988.

Freeman, R. Edward. *Corporate Strategy and the Search for Ethics*. Englewood Cliffs, NJ: Prentice-Hall, Inc., 1988.

Freudberg, David. *The Corporate Conscience: Money, Power and Responsible Business*. New York: AMACOM, 1986.

Friedman, Milton. "The Social Responsibility of Business to Increase Its Profits." *The New York Times Magazine*. September 13, 1970.

Friedrich, Otto. "The American Way of Debt." *Time*. May 31, 1982.

Garrett, Thomas M., and Richard J. Klonoski. *Business Ethics*, 2nd ed. Englewood Cliffs, NJ: Prentice-Hall, Inc., 1986.

Globe and Mail. Toronto, Ontario. August 12, 1985; February 15, 1988.

Godbold, Rea. "Life on the Receiving End." *Canadian Business*. Vol. 55, No. 6, June 1982.

Gram, Harold A. *The Christian Encounters Ethics and Social Responsibility in Business*. St. Louis: Concordia Publishing House, 1969.

Greiner, Larry E. "Evolution and Revolution as Organizations Grow." *Harvard Business Review*. July/August 1972.

Grenby, Mike. "There Is Life After Bankruptcy." *Abbotsford-Clearbrook Times*. Wednesday, July 27, 1988.

Grootenboer, Ed. *About Work and Unions*. Toronto: Christian Labour Association of Canada, 1984.

Harris, Ed. "Straight Talk About Why Businesses Fail—And How They Can Be Saved." *Canadian Business*, Vol. 53, No. 7, July 1980.

Harris, R. Laird, ed. *Theological Wordbook of the Old Testament*, Vol. 2. Chicago: Moody Press, 1980.

Hartzler, Robert. "Where Was God (When the Farm Failed)." *Mennonite Brethren Herald*. January 24, 1986.

Haughey, John C. *The Holy Use of Money*. New York: The Crossroad Publishing Co., 1989.

Hawkes, Cheryl. "Bankruptcy: The Best Medicine." *Canadian Business*. Vol. 54, No. 12, December 1981.

Heilbroner, Robert L. *The Making of Economic Society*, 6th ed. Englewood Cliffs, NJ: Prentice-Hall, Inc., 1980.

Henriques, Diana B. "Wall Street: Speculating on Bankruptcies," *The New York Times*. October 21, 1990. Section 3, p. 15.

Hess, J. Daniel. *Ethics in Business and Labour*. Scottdale, PA: Herald Press, 1977.

Holmes, Arthur F. *Ethics: Approaching Moral Decisions*. Downers Grove, IL: InterVarsity Press, 1984.

Honsberger, John D. "Corporate Failure Can Be Predicted." *CA Magazine*. June 1979.

Huizingh, Larry, and Wilson, Bernard. "Getting the (Bankruptcy) Act Together." *Canadian Banker and ICB Review*, Vol. 89, No. 1, February 1982.

"Jimmy Pattison: The Man Behind Expo '86." *Faith Today*. September 1986.

Johnson, Albert J. *A Christian's Guide to Family Finances*. Wheaton, IL: Victor Books, 1983.

Johnson, Harold L., "Can the Businessman Apply Christianity?" *Harvard Business Review: The Business of Ethics and Business*. Special collection of classic articles copyright various years from 1957 to 1986, volume no. 11043.

Jones, W. T. et al., editors. *Approaches to Ethics*, 2nd edition. New York: McGraw-Hill, 1969.

Journal of Business Ethics. Dordrecht: Kluwer Academic Publishers.

Kaiser, Walter C. *Toward an Exegetical Theology*. Grand Rapids: Baker Book House, 1981.

Kelly, Russell. *Pattison: Portrait of a Capitalist Superstar*. Vancouver, B.C.: New Star Books Ltd., 1986.

Kiechel III, Walter. "Unfuzzing Ethics for Managers." *Fortune*. November 23, 1987.

Kreider, Carl. *The Christian Entrepreneur*. Scottdale, PA: Herald Press, 1980.

Krutza, William J. "The Near-sighted Ethics of Christian Businessmen." *Eternity*. September 1976.

Krystal, Esther; Moran-Sackett, Marsha; Thompson, Sylvia V.; and Contoni, Lucille. "Serving the Unemployed." *Social Casework*, Vol. 64, No. 2, February 1981.

Kuyers, Milt. "Do Christ and Business Mix?" *The Banner*. Vol. 125, No. 19, May 14, 1990.

LaCroix, W. L. *Principles for Ethics in Business*. Washington: University Press of America, 1979.

LeMay, Tracy. "Management: The Key to Survival." *Financial Times*. April 26, 1982.

Lindsell, Harold. *Free Enterprise: A Judeo-Christian Defense*. Wheaton, IL: Tyndale House Publishers, Inc., 1982.

"Loser of the Month." *The Wittenburg Door*. No. 51, October/November, 1979.

Magliato, Joe. *The Wall Street Gospel*. Eugene, OR: Harvest House Publishers, 1981.

Manning, Preston. "Good News for Bad Times." Lecture given at Regent College, Vancouver, B.C., January 1983, available on audio cassette tape.

Martens, Elmer A. *Jeremiah*. Scottdale, PA: Herald Press, 1986.

Matthews, John B.; Goodpaster, Kenneth R.; and Nash, Laura L. *Policies and Persons*. New York: McGraw-Hill Book Company, 1985.

McCoy, Charles S. *Management of Values: The Ethical Difference in Corporate Policy and Performance*. Boston: Pitman, 1985.

Messer, Tom. "Canadian Bankruptcies Analyzed by Feds." *Canadian Building*. January/February 1983, Vol. 33, No. 1/2.

Meyer, Galen. "Jesus in the Office." *The Banner*. Vol. 125, No. 19, May 14, 1990.

Miller, Roger L. *Economic Issues for Consumers*, Sixth Edition. St. Paul: West Publishing Company, 1990.

Moran, John Jude. *Practical Business Law*. Englewood Cliffs, NJ: Prentice-Hall, Inc., 1985.

Morris, Leon. *The Gospel According to St. Luke*. Grand Rapids: Wm. B. Eerdmans, 1974.

Nash, Laura L. "Ethics without the sermon." *Harvard Business Review*. November-December, 1981.

Nelson, Benjamin. *The Idea of Usury*. Chicago: University of Chicago Press, 1969.

Paust, Jordan L.; Upp, Robert D.; and Sherry, John E. H. *Business Law*. Fourth Edition. St. Paul: West Publishing Co., 1984.

Peck, M. Scott. *The Road Less Traveled*. New York: Simon and Schuster, 1978.

Pemberton, Prentiss L., and Finn, Daniel Rush. *Toward a Christian Economic Ethic*. Minneapolis: Winston Press, Inc., 1985.

Platt, Harlan D. *Why Companies Fail: Strategies for Detaching, Avoiding, and Profiting from Bankruptcy*. Lexington, MA: C. C. Heath, 1985.

"Positive Power." *Money Matters*. Vol. 5, No. 1. Spring, 1988.

Power for Living. July 3, 1983. A publication of Scripture Press Publications, Inc., Glen Ellyn, IL.

Pritchard, James B. *Ancient Near Eastern Texts*. Princeton University Press, 1955.

Rawls, John. *A Theory of Justice*. Cambridge, MA: The Belknap Press of Harvard University Press, 1971.

Roebuck, Carl. *The World of Ancient Times*. New York: Charles Scribner's Sons, 1966.

Roels, Shirley J. "Ethics, Loneliness, and Business." *The Banner*. Vol. 125, No. 19, May 14, 1990.

Romain, Ken. "Lack of Management Skills Greases Skid to Bankruptcy." *Globe and Mail*. Friday, May 29, 1987.

Ryval, Michael. "Is Your Business Going for Broke?" *The Financial Post Magazine*. October 31, 1981.

Schaff, Philip, and Wace, Henry. *The Nicene and Post-Nicene Fathers*. Grand Rapids: Wm. B. Eerdmans, reprint.

Schaffer, Ulrich. *Greater Than Our Hearts*. New York: Harper and Row, 1981.

Siverd, Bonnie. *Count Your Change: A Woman's Guide to Sudden Financial Change*. New York: Priam Books, 1983.

Smedes, Lewis B. *Mere Morality*. Grand Rapids, MI: Wm. B. Eerdmans Publishing Co., 1983.

Smyth, J. E.; Soberman, D. A.; and Easson, A. J. *The Law and Business Administration in Canada*. Scarborough, ON: Prentice-Hall Canada, Inc., 1987.

Solomon, Robert C., and Hanson, Kristine R. *Above the Bottom Line: An Introduction to Business Ethics*. New York: Harcourt Brace Jovanovich, Inc., 1983.

Solomon, Robert C., and Hanson, Kristine. *It's Good Business*. New York: Atheneum, 1985.

Spohn, William C. *What Are They Saying About Scripture and Ethics?* New York: Paulist Press, 1984.

"Success Religion." *Testament*. A CBC radio series about the religious experience of today, produced by Don Mowatt and Katherine Carolan. July 3, 1983.

Sullivan, Teresa A.; Warren, Elizabeth and Westbrook Jay Lawrence. *As We Forgive Our Debtors: Bankruptcy and Consumer Credit in America.* New York: Oxford University Press, 1989.

Sutherland, John R. "The Ethics of Bankruptcy: A Biblical Perspective." *Journal of Business Ethics*. Vol. 7, No. 12, December 1988.

Sutherland, John R. "Usury: God's Forgotten Doctrine." *CRUX*. Vol. XVIII, No. 1, March 1982.

Sutherland, John R., and Ross B. Emmett. Book review of *Free Enterprise: A Judeo-Christian Defense*, by Harold Lindsell in *CRUX*. Vol. XIX, No. 2, June 1983.

Tassé, Roger; Hansberger, John D.; Carignana, Pierre; and Landry, Raymond A. *Report of the Study Committee on Bankruptcy and Insolvency Legislation*. Ottawa: Information Canada, 1970.

Taylor, Jack. "Business Failure: Why It Happens, and How to Avoid It Through Planning." *Small Business Review*. Vol. 3, No. 1, November 1982.

The Province. Vancouver, British Columbia, August 25, 1987.

The Sun. Vancouver, British Columbia. July 15, 1983; January 30, 1985; January 4, 1988.

Thompson, Robert V. *Unemployed*. Downers Grove, IL: InterVarsity Press, 1983.

Trott, Betty. "Ethics and the Executive: What Works Is Not Always Enough." *Executive*. April 1983.

Tuleja, Tad. *Beyond the Bottom Line*. New York: Facts on File Publications, 1985.

Van Dam, Cees, and Stallaert, Lund, editors. *Trends in Business Ethics*. Boston: Kluwer Boston Inc., 1978.

Velasquez, Manuel G. *Business Ethics*, 2nd edition. Englewood Cliffs, NJ: Prentice-Hall, Inc., 1988.

Von Rad, G. *Deuteronomy*. Philadelphia: Westminster Press, 1966.

Wall Street Journal. New York, NY. October 31-November 3, 1983.

Walsh, Sharon. "Bankruptcy Business Booms," *The Washington Post*. October 4, 1990. p. A1.

Wantuck, Mary-Margaret. "A Better Balance in Bankruptcy Law." *Nation's Business*. April 1985.

Wantuck, Mary-Margaret. "Keeping a Small Business Afloat." *Nation's Business*. April 1985.

Werhane, Patricia H. *Persons, Rights, and Corporation*. Englewood Cliffs, NJ: Prentice-Hall, Inc., 1985.

"Whatever Happened to Ethics." *Time*. May 25, 1987.

Willes, John A. *Contemporary Canadian Business Law*. Toronto: McGraw-Hill Ryerson, 1981.

Williams, Oliver F., and Houck, John W. *Full Value*. San Francisco: Harper and Row, Publishers, 1978.

Wilson, Bernard. "A Customer Saved Is a Customer Gained." *The Canadian Banker and ICB Review*. Vol. 86, No. 6, December 1979.

Wilson, Bernard. "Spotting the Danger Signals." *The Canadian Banker and ICB Review*. Vol. 86, No. 5, October 1979.

Wilson, Bernard R. "The Creditor's Crunch." *Canadian Business*. Vol. 46, No. 3, March 1983.

Wilson, Bernard. "The Last Resort." *The Canadian Banker and ICB Review*. Vol. 87, No. 3, June 1980.

Wolf, Harold A. *Personal Financial Planning*. Boston: Allyn and Bacon, 1989.

Yates, Richard A. *Business Law in Canada*, Second Edition. Scarborough, ON: Prentice-Hall Canada Inc., 1989.

Subject Index

Indexes by Richard A. Wiebe, Public Services Libraries, Trinity Western University.

Bankruptcy has not been used as a main heading. Search directly under the subject desired, e.g., causes of bankruptcy, emotional impact of bankruptcy, etc.

Scripture Index

The Author

John R. Sutherland was born in Belleville, Ontario. Like many Trenton High School graduates before him, he pursued university education at Queen's University in nearby Kingston, completing the M.B.A. in 1970. Three years as a steel industry marketing specialist followed.

Local church involvement in youth work made Sutherland want to improve his knowledge of the Bible. This led him and his expectant wife, Sharon (Martin) Sutherland, to Deerfield, Illinois. There he spent a year at Trinity Evangelical Divinity School and experienced the birth of their first child, Stephen.

For three years Sutherland taught marketing and management at the post-secondary level in Sudbury, northern Ontario (during which time daughter Julie was born). There he also hosted a weekly open-line radio program for young people.

In 1977 Sutherland returned to Illinois to work toward an M.A. in biblical studies. At the time, Trinity Western (Langley, British Columbia), Canada's largest Christian liberal arts university, needed a business professor. Sutherland's combination of seminary training and interest in integrating biblical principles and marketplace issues proved appropriate, and he joined the faculty in 1978.

He left in 1984 to serve as an administrator at Regent

College. He returned to Trinity in 1987 and is now Associate Professor of Ethics and Organizational Behavior, as well as Chair of the Division of Business and Economics.

Sutherland and his family attend West Abbottsford (B.C.) Mennonite Church, where he teaches an adult Bible class and does some lay preaching. He has served since 1983 as a member of the Abbotsford School District Board of School Trustees.